Language & Literature Series

GENERAL EDITOR C. T. ONIONS

Persian Literature

an introduction

by

REUBEN LEVY, M.A.
LECTURER IN PERSIAN IN THE UNIVERSITY OF OXFORD

LONDON
OXFORD UNIVERSITY PRESS
Humphrey Milford
1923

Oxford University Press

London Edinburgh Glasgow Copenhagen
New York Toronto Melbourne Cape Town
Bombay Calcutta Madras Shanghai

Humphrey Milford Publisher to the UNIVERSITY

Printed in England

CONTENTS

The system of transliteration employed in the book is as follows:

ا = ’ [not represented at the beginning of a word].
ب = b
پ = p
ت = t
ث = s̤
ج = j
چ = ch
ح = ḥ
خ = kh
د = d
ذ = z̲
ر = r
ز = z
ژ = zh
س = s
ش = sh
ص = ṣ
ض = ẓ
ط = ṭ
ظ = z̤
ع = ‘
غ = gh
ف = f
ق = ḳ
ك = k
گ = g
ل = l
م = m
ن = n
و = w
ه = h
ى = y

ʹ indicates a long vowel.

From Cyrus the Great to the Islamic Conquest

THE people who inhabit Írán belong to the great Indo-European family, and their name 'Iranians' bears etymological affinity with the appellation 'Aryan'. The name 'Persia' is due to an accident of history that made the province of Párs or Fárs, the Greek 'Persis', predominant in Írán at the time when the attention of the Greeks was directed towards it. The language of the Iranians has marked affinities on the one hand with the languages akin to the classical tongues of Europe and on the other hand with the Sanskritic group of Indian languages. The Iranian group of nations, namely Persians, Medes, and others, have not always occupied the lands historically associated with their names. They seem in the course of their migrations to have separated from the parent stock somewhere in the region of the Caspian Sea, and wandered southwards through the country of the Oxus and the Jaxartes to their more recent home, where their history falls into well-marked periods.

Though there are legends which talk of an Iranian dynasty of Bactria in the dimmest past, yet the earliest historical reference to an Iranian state dates from about the middle of the ninth century B.C., when the territory of the Medes began to attract the attention of the Assyrian kings. Persia itself sprang into prominence with the appearance of Cyrus the Great, who reigned from 558–530 B.C. He overthrew the Median dynasty that then held supremacy, made himself master of Babylon with all its dependencies, and founded the Achaemenian dynasty, which took its origin in the province of Párs, and gave it such importance that, for the Greeks, Persis stood for the whole of Írán, as its latinized form 'Persia' does for us at the present day.

Cyrus was succeeded by his son Cambyses, who undertook to enlarge the empire left by his father and to conquer Egypt. He was recalled from his Egyptian expedition by a rebellion at home, led by one Gaumata, a Magian pretender, who assumed the character of the king's brother Smerdis, whom Cambyses had years before put to death on a suspicion of disloyalty. Cambyses was hastening home to crush the usurper when he died in Syria on the way, 521 B.C.

The next heir to the throne was Hystaspes who, like Cyrus, was a descendant of Achaemenes, the eponymous ancestor of the dynasty. But Hystaspes was either unwilling or unable to assert his right to the throne upon which the usurper had established himself strongly. It was therefore left for his son Darius to dislodge the pseudo-Smerdis and make himself king.

Darius came to the throne in 521 B.C., and from that date until his death in 485 B.C. was constantly engaged in campaigning, either in pursuit of fresh conquests, or in subjugating rebellious provinces. Persian literature may be said to begin with Darius. His own records of his campaigns have survived in inscriptions engraved in the Old Persian character upon various rocks and one or two stone monuments. The greatest and most important of the inscriptions is engraved upon the mighty rock of Bahistún, which lies about thirty miles east of Kirmánsháh on the Khurásán highway. Darius sets down in it his ancestry and titles, and describes in detail his exploits during the process of consolidating his throne. He acknowledges that it is by the grace of the supreme god Ahura Mazda that he has achieved his aims, and he calls down the god's blessing upon them that proclaim the contents of his record, and his curse upon them that would destroy or conceal it.

The inscription scarcely conforms to the accepted definition of literature as being either poetry or artistic prose, for its style is rough and abrupt, repetitions are many, and nearly every paragraph begins with the fixed formula, 'Says Darius the King', which produces the formal impression of a legal document.[1]

The following extract gives some indication of the character of the monument:

'Says Darius the king: This (is) what was done by me in Babylon.

Says Darius the king: This (is) what I did; by the grace of Ahura Mazda in the same year after that I became king I engaged in nineteen battles; by the grace of Ahura Mazda I waged them and seized nine kings; there was one, Gaumata by name, a Magian; he lied; thus he said: I am Bardiya the son of Cyrus; he made Persia rebellious ...; there was one Nidintu-Bél by name, a Babylonian; he lied; thus he said: I am Nebuchadrezzar the son of Nabú-na'id; he made Babylon rebellious ...

Says Darius the king: These nine kings I seized within these battles.

Says Darius the king: These are the provinces which became rebellious; the lie made them rebellious so that these deceived the people; afterwards Ahura Mazda gave them into my hand; as was my will so [I did] unto them ...

Says Darius the king: By the grace of Ahura Mazda much else (was) done by me that (is) not written on this inscription; for this reason it (is) not written lest whoever shall examine this inscription in the future, to him what has been done by me should seem too much, lest he be not convinced and think (it) false.

Nevertheless this and other inscriptions of Darius and those of his successors, Xerxes (Ahasuerus of the Bible, 485-465 B.C.) and Artaxerxes (465-424 B.C.), at Nakshi

[1] The history of the decipherment of the inscription is one of the marvels of philology. The first successful efforts were made by Grotefend in 1802, both the language and the script being then unknown quantities to him. He set to work by comparing two short parallel pieces and noting the differences which, on the basis of some earlier researches, he conjectured to be the names of the kings Darius and Xerxes. His conjectures proved correct, but the help thereby gained did not enable him to solve the whole of the cipher. The honour of the final decipherment rests with Sir Henry Rawlinson, who himself visited and at great personal risk copied the inscriptions on the almost inaccessible rock of Bahistún. L. W. King and R. C. Thompson of the British Museum ascended the rock and recopied the inscriptions in 1904.

Rustam and Persepolis, mark a definite beginning of national literature, though it may be doubted whether the mystery of letters was widely revealed among the people of Írán. They, in the Achaemenian period, were a hardy race, who extorted the respect of their contemporaries for their courage, temperance, and love of truth. Their king Cyrus was, to the Hebrews, the 'anointed of God', while the manly qualities of his subjects roused the admiration of the Greeks. Their records are such as might be expected from a race of warriors, terse and to the point, without any trace of poetic or emotional colouring. But they contain religious references such as the mention of Ahura Mazda, which are noteworthy as indicating that the king, and doubtless some of his subjects, were firm adherents of Zoroastrianism, and that the faith was then well established. The religious books of Zoroastrianism made a separate body of writings, which are included philologically in the Old Persian group.

The origin and date of the religion of Zoroaster have been subjects of great controversy. The very existence of Zoroaster himself has been denied, and his date has been put anywhere between 6,000 and 600 B.C. by those who maintain his reality. Modern scholarship for the most part favours the view that he flourished during the latter half of the seventh century B.C., probably in the region of the modern Azarbayján. It is a matter of dispute whether any religious or literary work of his has survived. Among the books which make up the *Avesta*, the Bible of Zoroastrianism, only a fragment, the 'Gáthás', or 'Psalms' is generally regarded as a possible work of the founder of the faith himself. The style of these psalms indicates that they were probably first declaimed from the rostrum, as may be seen from the following section taken from L. H. Mills's translation of prayer 43 in the Yasna (Holy Day liturgy).

Salvation to this man, salvation to him whosoever he may be! Let the absolutely ruling Great Creator grant us, He the living

Lord, the two eternal powers. Yea, verily, I ask it of Thee (O Ahura) for the maintaining of righteousness. And mayst Thou also give it to me (O inspiring) Piety, splendour as it is, holy blessings, the Good Mind's life.

Yea, to this one may the man endowed with glory give that best of all things, the (spiritual) glory. And do Thou likewise (Thyself) reveal Thine own (gifts) through Thy most bountiful spirit, O Mazda. (And do Thou teach us) Thy wonderful thoughts of wisdom, those of Thy Good Mind, which Thou hast revealed (to us) by Thy Righteousness (within us) with the happy increase of (our joy) and on a long life's every day. . . .

(For) so I conceived of Thee as bountiful, O Great Giver, Mazda, when I beheld Thee as supreme in the generation of life, when, as rewarding deeds and words, Thou didst establish evil for the evil, and happy blessings for the good, by Thy (great) virtue (to be adjudged to each) in the creation's final change.

Professor A. V. Williams Jackson, who has made the Avesta his special study, sees real poetry in some of the Yashts of the Avesta. He quotes in support of this a section from the Yasht in praise of Mithra :

Mithra, the celestial angel,
Foremost climbeth Mount Haraiti (Alburz)
In advance of the sun immortal,
Which is drawn by fleeting coursers.
He, the first, in gold adornment
Grasps the beauteous lofty summits ;
Thence beneficent he glanceth
Over all the Aryan homeland,
Where the valiant chiefs in battle
Range their troops in countless numbers.[1]

The origin of the whole Avesta and the authorship of the various books are as much matters of debate as the history of Zoroaster himself. 'Avesta', which is a name applied not only to the whole text of the work, but also nowadays to the dialect in which it is written, is a language closely akin to Sanskrit, and varies in many points from the Old Persian of the cuneiform inscriptions. Some scholars have indeed regarded the language of the Avesta as Eastern Persian and that of the inscriptions as Western Persian, but the theory does not admit of proof.

What we now possess of the Avesta is only a fragment of

[1] A. V. W. Jackson, *Early Persian Poetry*, New York, 1920.

the original which, according to Parsi tradition, consisted, in Sasanian times, of twenty-one books. Of these only one whole book and various incomplete portions have come down to modern days, and they form a corpus of liturgical compositions and ecclesiastical laws which owes its preservation to its use in public worship. It is divided into two parts, the Avesta proper and the Khurda Avesta, or Little Avesta—which is a book of short prayers. The Avesta itself contains three main divisions: (1) the Vendídád, which traditionally is the only complete book, and which is a compilation of religious laws, mythical tales, and 'Gáthás'; (2) the Visperad, which is a collection of sacrificial litanies; and finally, (3) the Yasna, which is another liturgical work. Except to the professed student of Zoroastrianism the value of the Avesta lies in its philological rather than its literary interest, which is no greater than that of the Levitical portions of the Pentateuch.

Alexander the Great's conquest of Persia in 331 B.C. not only put an end to the Achaemenian dynasty but also dealt a heavy blow at its religion. To judge from the remains of the period the conquest crushed both national spirit and religious enthusiasm, and, for the long period of five and a half centuries after it, prophets, poets, and historians were either uninspired or have been lost to posterity through the total disappearance of their works. It was not until A.D. 224, when the Sasanian dynasty was founded, that a revival of literary production took place.

In the meantime, as may be gathered from the classical historians of Greece and Rome and from the coins minted by Alexander's successors, the conqueror's empire was divided up amongst his generals Seleucus and Archelaus, who ruled their provinces as satraps. In the troubled years which followed, two dynasties came to the fore in the constant struggles for supremacy. These were the Seleucid dynasty of Mesopotamia and the Arsacid of Parthia, whose histories are inextricably bound up with that of the Roman Empire.

The ultimate decline of Parthian power helped the beginnings of a Persian national movement of revolt against Western influences; it coincided with a revival of Zoroastrianism which had had for centuries to share its influence with paganism, Judaism, and probably Christianity. The renaissance of the national spirit found expression in A.D. 226 in the founding of the Sasanian dynasty, a line of native Iranian princes, of whom the first, Ardashír or Artakhshír (in graecized form, Artaxerxes), traced his descent from the Achaemenians.

The language of Persia had by this time undergone considerable modification, though Zoroastrianism and the Avesta had helped to preserve many of its characteristics. In the stage which it had then reached, it is known as 'Pahlawi', which is a phonetic modification of 'Parthawi'; i.e. 'Parthian'. Pahlawi was not the language of the Parthians, but just as Persis in earlier days became representative of the whole of Írán, so during the centuries when Parthia dominated Írán, Iranian and Parthian became practically synonymous terms.

The earliest pieces of writing in Pahlawi are certain rock inscriptions, consisting merely of names or titles, or of small fragments of historical records dating from early Sasanian times. Between the date of these inscriptions and the Arab invasion of Persia there must have been considerable production of Pahlawi literature, particularly on subjects connected with Zoroastrianism. The destructiveness of the Muslim conquest would, however, account for the disappearance of many works, while the imposition of the Arabic alphabet on the newly converted Muslims of the invaded land, confined the use and knowledge of the complicated

Pahlawi character almost exclusively to the Zoroastrian priesthood. Islam, moreover, would scarcely have looked favourably on the publication of any 'Gabr' or 'Fire-worshipping' work which might controvert its influence, and in fact little was produced after the ninth century A.D. For the preservation of the comparatively few Pahlawi works which survived, we are indebted to the Parsis of Bombay, the cultured descendants of the Persian Zoroastrians, who were compelled to flee to India in the eighth century A.D. to escape the rigours of Islam. Although the emigrants themselves did not carry with them or preserve much of Pahlawi interest, yet later importations from Persia by the Parsi priests saved a number of works which might otherwise have perished.

What survives in Pahlawi owes its preservation to its religious character or to its connexion with the Avesta, which is invariably accompanied by the 'Zand', i.e. 'the commentary'. The Zand itself is written in Pahlawi, and Avesta and Zand correspond practically to scripture and interpretation. Pahlawi translations of the Avesta and various technical works on the doctrines, practices, and cosmogony of Magianism, make up the balance of specifically religious books. Of these the best known in Europe are the *Bundahish*, the *Dínkart*, and the *Mainyo i Khirad*, which have been made available in translations by E. W. West and others.

It is, however, the small secular portion of Pahlawi literature that has been preserved along with the rest, that is of specific importance in the study of the development of subsequent Persian writings, for in it there begin to appear the particular ideas, legends, and historical materials used by the poets of Islamic Persia. An amazing variety of subjects is dealt with in the small number of texts which have survived. Amongst them are a large fragment of

A Social Code of the Parsis in Sasanian Times, practically a code of personal laws connected with marriage, personal property, slaves, &c.; a manual of *Forms for Letter Writing*, giving suitable beginnings and endings for use in polite or official correspondence; and a glossary of Old Pahlawi into Pázand. There are also a fanciful *History of Chess*, and the *Tale of Khusraw i Kawátán and his Page*. But of the greatest immediate interest are the *Yátkár i Zarírán* (The Memoir of the Zarírs), also called the *Sháh-náma i Gushtásp* (The Epic of Gushtásp), and the *Kárnámak i Artakhshír i Pápakán* (The Book of Mighty Deeds of Ardashír, Son of Bábak). Both of these deal with legendary or semi-historical personages of early Persian story, and contain much that resembles the legends which the poet Firdawsí employed in his *Sháh-náma*, the great 'Epic of kings'.

The *Yátkár* is an account of the war which breaks out between the two monarchs Arjásp and Gushtásp, when the latter refuses to give up his newly assumed Zoroastrianism at the bidding of Arjásp's envoys. Zarír, Gushtásp's brother, who was responsible for the defiance of Arjásp, after performing prodigies of valour in the battle, is finally slain, but his efforts bring victory to his side.

The *Kárnámak i Artakhshír* contains even greater resemblances to the *Sháh-náma* of Firdawsí than the *Yátkár*. The legend relates the adventures of Ardashír, who is the son of Sásán, and whose mother is the daughter of a 'lord of the marches' named Bábak. Sásán, though apparently a humble shepherd, is really a descendant of Darius, and his son Ardashír, when of age, is summoned to court by the paramount king of Persia. Thence he is banished for quarrelling with the king's son, but gaining power, he returns and succeeds in overthrowing the king and marrying his daughter. The hero's further adventures take up the remainder of the account.

The exact date of these compositions is unknown, but they were with little doubt the product of the generosity of one of the later Sasanian princes. Daḳíḳí, who began the famous *Sháh-náma* (Book of Kings) and Firdawsí, who completed it, seem to have made extensive use of this material. It is true that there are differences; the style of the original is simple and the action of the story moves forward directly and without digression, while the *Sháh-náma* makes constant excursions from the path of the story, and its style is overloaded with ornamental superfluities. Also the two versions differ in their ending; nevertheless the resemblances are great enough to justify the conclusion that the two are interdependent.

Of Sasanian poetry nothing has been preserved, and though it seems strange that monarchs of the standing of Núshírwán or Khusraw Parwíz should have had no minstrels or poets to sing their praises, yet it is possible that Sasanian art found its expression in architecture and sculpture rather than in letters.

In the year A.D. 651 the empire of the Sasanians was brought to an end by the Arabian invasion of Persia and the defeat of Yazdigird, the last member of the dynasty. Throughout the whole of the history of Arabia periods of dearth have been followed by migrations of the inhabitants of the country to more fertile lands. The last wave of migration coincided with the rise of Islam, which gathered strength as the Arab conquests proceeded. When in Persia a series of unexpectedly easy victories was followed by a period of resistance from the less accessible strongholds of Iranian civilization, the Arabian corporate feeling aroused by this opposition began to identify itself with the new faith revealed by the Arab Muhammad. What had been loose migration of tribes now became a series of organized campaigns to crush opposition to the Arabs and to their newly acquired beliefs. The ancient religion of Persia, Zoroastrianism, was compelled to give way to the overwhelming force of the Arab doctrines, and what had once been a great empire was reduced to a tributary province.

It is not possible to estimate to the full the effects of this great external cataclysm upon the nation. Islam, like Judaism, affects to regulate every moment of the lives of its adherents, and a new outlook on the things of this world and the next was its inevitable consequence. It changed the whole system of the theological references of the nation, and hence a large part of its literary relations too. The Pahlawi script was forced to give way to the Arabic, and a knowledge of the Arabic tongue became indispensable to the converts, for religious worship and the correct reading of the Ḳur'án, their new Bible, were impossible without it.

The yielding and adaptable nature of the Persians did not help them to make any decisive opposition to the physical and political power which attempted to crush them. But the very adaptability of the people and their resilience of character preserved some of the elements of their spiritual being and gave promise of new life. Zoroastrianism was not entirely wiped out, though it was incapable of expansion, and the legends, tales and folk-lore of earlier days survived, to become the basis of future literature. Islam itself became coloured in Persia with the patriotic feeling that gave rise to the faction or 'Shí'a', which came into being after the death of 'Alí.

Little is known of the internal condition of Persia during the first century and a half of Arab rule. Politically the whole of Persia was held in subjection as a tributary province, whose doings were strictly supervised by an intelligence system devised by the first Umayyad caliph. It is not probable, therefore, that any local literature in the form of patriotic compositions received encouragement, while works of other kinds would, on the principle attributed to 'Umar, be destroyed as unnecessary and superfluous, seeing that the Ḳur'án was the pure fount of all knowledge. But even the conquering nation during the first century of campaigning and organization produced little or nothing of literary value. If any poetry was composed, it was on the old pagan models, and celebrated in stereotyped fashion the poet's amatory adventures rather than the victories of Islam. The silence of Persia under the circumstances becomes the more comprehensible thereby.

The Period of the 'Abbásid Caliphate
A.D. 750-1258

THE opposition to the Umayyads, which had been displayed by orthodox Muslims and by the descendants of the Prophet's relatives who pretended to the Caliphate, gradually gathered strength. With great cunning the leaders of the movement took advantage of the discontent of the oppressed Persians, as well as of their religious hostility to the existing Caliphate, and roused them to aid in revolution. When the movement was finally successful and the capital of the Muslim Empire moved from Damascus to Baghdad, Persia acquired a position of importance in the state, and her inhabitants provided many of its great officers, amongst whom the Barmecides are the best known.

Arabic remained the official language of state correspondence and also of theology and science, with the result that though many of the eminent scientists and theologians of Islam were Persians, their writings belong rather to Arabic literature than to Persian. The great number of Persians who made a name by their writings in Arabic must, however, be taken into consideration when an estimate of the

Iranian genius is being made. Ṭabarí in the realm of history, Avicenna in medicine and philosophy, al Bírúní in chronology, and al Bayẓáwí in Ḳur'ánic interpretation are but a few of the natives of Iran whose fame rests on their scientific works in Arabic. One Persian, Ibn Khurdádbih, is credited with the oldest geographical work extant in Arabic, the *Kitábu 'l Masálik wa 'l Mamálik* (Book of the Roads and Countries) which was completed in A. D. 844.

In their own language there remained for Persians the art of poetical composition. Even here they at first imitated and borrowed the forms of Arabic poetry. It was an adoption which was but natural, seeing that Khurásán and Transoxiana, usually considered the cradle of modern Persian literature, were for more than three centuries governed by Arabs. But the borrowed metres were for the most part adapted and changed, new forms were added and the conquered Persians finally succeeded in excelling their Arab teachers in poetic skill; for it is a quality of theirs that they are capable of visualizing anew and improving their borrowings from other peoples, in art as well as in religion.

It was not, however, until the authority of the Caliphs of Baghdad had so far weakened as to allow independent dynasties to be set up in distant parts of the empire, that poetical composition became common in Persia. The first of such independent dynasties in that country was founded by one Ṭáhir ibn Ḥusayn in A. D. 820. He was an Arab general who had been granted the governorship of Khurásán in return for military aid given to Ma'mún, the son of Hárún al Rashíd, in his battles against his brother Amín. Ṭáhir handed on his powers to his son and so established the Ṭáhirid line (A. D. 820–72), whose members with their Arab tradition behind them could scarcely have had much sympathy with the works inspired by native feeling or tradition. The names of two poets only have reached us from those days, Ḥanzala of Bádaghís and Maḥmúdi Warráḳ of Harát, both of whom continued into the days of the Ṣaffárid, or 'Coppersmith' dynasty (A.D. 867–903) which displaced the Ṭáhirids.

Real progress only began in the days of the Sámánids, (A.D. 874–999). These princes belonged to a warlike line who traced their origin to the Sasanians. They proved their soldierly qualities by taking possession of their native province of Transoxiana, also by their conquest of Khurásán and of a large part of north-eastern Persia, which they seized after defeating the last of the Ṣaffárids (A.D. 900). With all their campaigning they found time to concern themselves with art and letters, and gathered round them a brilliant company of poets and historians to sing their praises and chronicle their victories. The biographers preserve the names and occasionally the verses of minstrels who lived in those early days.

Amongst the clients and encomiasts of the Sámánids was one Abú Shukúr of Balkh, (fl. c. A.D. 950), who is said to have been the first to compose in the Rubá'í, or quatrain form, of which great use was made in later centuries for mystical verse. Fragments of his compositions displaying refreshing simplicity of style are to be found in the biographical and lexicographical dictionaries. These are constantly being compiled in Islamic countries, and they are valuable sources for the early history of Persian literature. The biographers usually quote extracts from the poets with whom they are dealing, while the lexicographers often support their reading of a word by a poetic quotation.

Somewhat later than Abú Shukúr was Rúdagí, the first great classical poet of Persia († c. A.D. 954). With him began what may be called the court poetry of Írán. It was in the main a system of panegyrics filled with hyperbole and exaggerated flattery, composed by versifiers in return for the practical goodwill of their patrons, who not only saved many from immediate starvation and certain obscurity, but were ready to reward particularly pleasing work with valuable gifts. Rúdagí's real name was Abú Abdilláh Ja'far bin Muḥammad, and his 'takhallus' (pen-name), 'Rúdagí', was taken from the name of his birthplace in Khurásán. Tradition says that he was born blind, but that in spite of this defect his brilliant talents made him the favourite and court poet of the Sámánid monarch Naṣr ibn Aḥmad (fl. A.D. 914–43). His style is simple and direct and gives evidence of sincerity of feeling, though there are already apparent in it touches of the artificiality and floweriness of diction which marred much of the later poetry. An often-quoted story tells that he composed a lyric so exquisite in its word painting that it succeeded in convincing his patron where the arguments of many courtiers had failed. The Prince had made a long stay at Harát, and the persuasions of his courtiers, who pined for their native Bukhárá, proved unavailing until they called the poet to their aid. The Prince's eagerness to return was then so keenly aroused that he leapt upon his horse and rode off without waiting to put on his boots. The poem which brought about this object has been criticized by later biographers on the score that it was so lacking in art as not to be poetry. The criticism indicates what it was that led to the later artificiality and elaborateness of style.

With Rúdagí one begins to notice the conflict, so prominent in later literature, between the promptings of natural pleasures traditional in Persia with the rigid theological system of the Arabs that tried to curb them. Woman, wine, and song would not be suppressed by theology, and songs in praise of them gave spontaneous expression to the poet's emotions. In later life Rúdagí lost the favour of his patron and died in poverty. His work, which was of prodigious extent, included three historical romances, of which the best known, *Wámak and 'Azrá*, was based on Pahlawi materials and found many imitators and adaptors. None of these romantic poems has survived, but a fair number of his panegyrics and odes have been preserved in biographical works and anthologies. The fragmentary eulogy that follows gives some indication of his methods in that *genre*.

Whenever foeman dreams of strife with thee,
Before thy sword his limbs part in dismay,
Thy law joins finch and hawk in friendly flight
Thy stern behest leagueth each night with day.
Live joyously, for now the wind of fate
Of calumny hath rooted up the tree.
Ever, while name or sign of earth remains,
While high heaven remains sublime for thee,
Let all thy friends rejoice with feast and song,
Let them that envy be cast down with grief.

Another effort, of which the translation attempts to preserve the original rhythm, shows the poet in a more epigrammatic vein:

Thy retainers in a battle are as tailors on the field—
Though a tailor, lord of empires, thou would'st never find with them—
For their lances on thy foemen as a measure they do wield,
What they cut out with their sword-blades with their arrows they do hem.

One of Rúdagí's odes to wine is quoted by Jámí in the *Bahāristán*. Professor Browne, in his *Literary History of Persia*, has reprinted a translation of it by the late Professor Cowell, of which the first couplet is:

Bring me yon wine which thou might'st call a melted ruby in its cup,
Or like a scimitar unsheathed, in the sun's noontide light held up.

Another ode, on spring, seems worth translation:

April's moon with winter hath done battle,
And dust pollutes the air o'er fields blood-red;
Tears from April-clouds the branches broider,
The scented air imbues the earth with musk.
Thou hast concealed, Lord, what Time disclosed,
And Korah brought to light what man had hid.
Like Laylá smiles the tulip on the field,
With Majnún's eye the cloud rains tears on earth.

From each hour's fount rose-water scented flows,
Wherein my love doth lave her rosy cheek.
Let one lock stray and hundred hearts go free,
At one cold glance two hundred hearts are grieved.

Another poet who flourished in the encouraging atmosphere of the Sámánid court was Daḳíḳí, whose name has already been mentioned in connexion with the Pahlawi *Yátkár*. Of his life little is known for certain. He is said to have been a Zoroastrian by some scholars, who base their statement on one of his lyrics which gives the poet's view of the world's four choicest blessings as ruby lips, the music of the harp, Zoroaster's teaching, and red wine. The conjunction of Zoroastrianism with the conventional hedonisms may, however, be merely a touch of the antiquary appearing in the poet. In any case there is little or no foundation but this verse for the assumption that the poet was anything but a Muslim, which, to judge from other facts, he probably was. He is best known to fame for having undertaken to set into the epic form of the *Sháh-náma* the ancient Iranian materials that he had collected for his patron. But he had only completed a thousand verses when he was murdered by a slave. We are indebted for knowledge of this fact to the poet Firdawsí who completed the enormous work of the *Sháh-náma* which is usually, and deservedly, known as his. But for Firdawsí's statement it would not have been obvious that he had borrowed Daḳíḳí's verses, the style and diction of the two poets being indistinguishable.

The *Sháh-náma* may properly be considered a product of the patronage of the Sámánids in whose time it was composed and to one of whom it was first offered. The encouragement of these princes was not confined to poets. Prince Manṣúr ibn Núḥ the Sámánid had for his vizier al Bal'amí, the translator of Ṭabarí's *Universal History* from Arabic into Persian. The translation, which is somewhat abridged from the original, is the earliest piece of connected prose in modern Persian. The Arabic original itself is an example of the Iranian genius, for its author Ṭabarí was born in, and derived his pen-name from, Ṭabaristán, the province which lay along the south shore of the Caspian Sea. Moreover, two great physicians and philosophers, Rhazes and Avicenna, made their reputations under the Sámánids. To one of the latter, Abú Sáliḥ Manṣúr, Governor of Khurásán, Rhazes dedicated a treatise on medicine which he had written in Arabic and which he called, after the prince, *Kitáb i Manṣúri.*

Contemporary with the House of Sámán there existed a hardy stronghold of Shí'ism in Ṭabaristán and Gurgán under the 'Alids (A.D. 864–920) and Ziyárids (A.D. 928–1042). Of the latter one at least, Ḳábús ibn Washmgír, († A.D. 1012) was an accomplished poet, as well as a friend of poets. But he is best known to fame for having given sanctuary to Avicenna when the latter fled to escape the clutches of the acquisitive Sultan Maḥmúd of Ghazna. This prince had in A.D. 998 inherited from his father Sabuktagín, a Turk who commenced life as a slave, a small kingdom which had Ghazna for its capital. Around this nucleus he built up by conquest, with incredible speed, an empire which stretched from Lahore to Isfahán and dominated Baghdad itself. In the course of his campaigns he overthrew not only the Sámánids, but robbed the Buwayhids, who were then dominant in Baghdad and western Persia, of a large portion of their domains. The Buwayhids were a Persian and Shí'a family who took their origin in the province of Daylam, south-west of the Caspian Sea, and who through their military prowess had, by the middle of the tenth century, made themselves supreme in the Caliphate. Through Maḥmúd's victories they were dealt a blow from which they were never able to recover, and they finally succumbed to the same power that in due course overthrew the Ghaznawí dynasty, namely the Turkoman tribe of Saljúḳs.

Maḥmúd in the heyday of his power gathered around him at Ghazna a company of poets and scientists which became famous in the history of Persian literature. His poet-laureate 'Unṣurí of Balkh († c. 1050) has left a *díwán*, or collection of poems put together according to the alphabetical order of the rhymes, which contains some moderately good poetry in various forms. For the most part, however, it consists of long panegyrics in the most verbose style celebrating the magnificence of the Sultan's victories and recording the poet's gratitude for favours received at his hands. In this the work is typical of that of most contemporary and later panegyrists, who attempted to imitate Rúdagí but never succeeded in achieving his simplicity of style or beauty of diction. A couplet from one of 'Unṣurí's panegyrics and part of an ode in the 'question and answer' style are quoted for purposes of illustration.

Let him bind or let him loosen, let him take or let him give,
While the earth stands on its pillar let our king have this device :—
What he takes becomes an empire, what he gives is treasure rare,
What he binds is feet of foemen, what he loosens, fortress fast.

Said I : Make but a sign with that ravishing small mouth of thine.
Said she : In this world below there never can be such a sign.
Said I : From thy garden would I gladly cull a posy gay.
Said she : From my garden not a flower can be torn away.
Said I : Sweetheart, grievous loss hath come to me from thine embrace.
Said she : 'Tis for profit that such loss afflicts the human race.

With 'Unṣurí were the poets Farrukhí and 'Asjadí, both of whom belonged to his school of poetical composition, though Farrukhí's work contains much more real poetry than that of his teacher 'Unṣurí. A somewhat later follower of the panegyric art was Minuchihrí of Dámghán who was court poet to Maḥmúd's successors as well as to the great conqueror. He died soon after A.D. 1041 leaving a *díwán* composed mainly of eulogistic *ḳaṣídas* and of odes bacchic or erotic.

Maḥmúd's panegyrists 'Unṣurí, Farrukhí, and the rest belonged to a class whose existence depended upon the generosity of their patrons and whose compositions were moulded specifically to flatter. The worth of their work as literature can be estimated accordingly. The standard form for panegyric, as also for satire, was the *ḳaṣída* (Elegiac form) which was borrowed from the Arabic and consisted of ten or more—usually many more—verses, all with the same rhyme, a restriction not conducive to good poetry. Interested concern in the panegyrics was even in their author's own day naturally enough confined to those who were the objects of their praises, but as examples of skill in verse composition they still have a historical interest.

Two members of Maḥmúd's 'entourage' stand far in front of all his panegyrists for poetical genius, namely Asadí and his famous pupil Firdawsí. Asadí, who died between A.D. 1030 and 1041, having then outlived his pupil, was the originator of a class of poems known as *munáẕara* (disputation or repartee poems) which serve as introductions to eulogies, and in which imaginary characters vie with each other in describing the perfections of the object of praise. The scope of such poems was in later times extended to include mystical subjects, a well-known example being 'Árifí's *Gúy u Chawgán* (The Ball and the Polo-stick).

Of the poets, however, at the Ghaznawí capital Firdawsí has made the deepest impression on the literature of his native land. He had come to Maḥmúd, then the most powerful monarch of the Islamic world, bringing with him his *Sháh-náma*, the result of thirty-five years labour, in the hope of receiving adequate reward for his efforts. The story of his disappointment, of his satire of Maḥmúd and subsequent flight, has been often repeated by the biographers and is well known. The satire, which is not ordinarily incorporated with the *Sháh-náma*, has been handed down in a number of versions differing widely in length. But however small a portion of what we have is considered genuine, the spirit of the composition was such as to make it prudent for the poet to be at a safe distance when it was delivered to its victim. A far less tyrannous and 'touchy' sovereign than Maḥmúd would have been roused to anger by its shafts; as, for example, by this:

Were not the emperor so meanly disposed,
To proud rank and station would he exalt me.
And learning is foreign of aspect to him,
Or else he had set me aloft on a throne.
His ancestors never were wearers of crowns,
No plan had he therefore of how kings behave.
Had but the Sháh had a Sháh for his father,
With a golden crown he had adorned my head.
If she had been a royal queen that bore him,
Knee-deep in gold and silver he had set me.
But, since greatness in his pedigree is not,
Great names with him can find no fair approval.

or by this:

No slave-girl's son can ever gain perfection,
Though amongst his sires be conquerors galore.

Legend says that in the end the Sultan forgave the poet and sent him presents befitting his worth, but they only arrived when Firdawsí's body was being carried to the grave. Jámí has rightly judged Maḥmúd's fate in history:

Maḥmúd's splendour and pomp are departed,
And naught of his story lingers on earth
But this, that he slighted mighty Firdawsí,
Being in ignorance blind to his worth.

The *Sháh-náma* incorporates most of the heroic legends of early Írán. These had been used before in a prose setting, and probably also in versified attempts which have not come down to us. Firdawsí's poem, however, by the extent and wealth of its contents, was marked out for greatness, and the ardent patriotism which it breathes made it the national epic of the Persians. Though in the poet's own day his high estimate of Zoroastrian heroes gained him the hatred of the more fanatical Muslims, the praise bestowed in the preface upon 'Alí, the beloved of the Shí'a, soon outbalanced that to which they had laid objection.

The material which the poet uses is immense. It begins with the earliest heroes of Iranian antiquity, the three princes, Guyúmart, Húshang, and Tahmúrath, who first brought knowledge on earth, and ends with a short account of the Sasanian dynasty and a description of the death of Yazdigird III, the last of his line. In the course of the poem the lives of fifty kings are recounted, together with innumerable narratives of heroic adventure. Some of these are devoted to the subject of the many wars between Írán and Turán which are symbolical of the long conflict between Persia and Turkey. One incident related is the famous story of Suhráb and Rustam, familiar to English readers from Matthew Arnold's poem *Sohrab and Rustum*; and a curious legend, also included by the poet, saves national pride by asserting that Alexander the Great had a Persian princess for his mother.

The inordinate length of the poem, its monotonous metre and constant repetitions must be accounted defects. Its stereotyped descriptions of characters and scenes present no clear-cut pictures to the mind, and its lack of historical perspective is a grave fault. But to the Persian it is the subject matter of the epic and not its style that counts, and its popularity is proved by the innumerable imitations which have followed, though never equalled, the work.

It is said that towards the end of his life Firdawsí, disturbed by the disapproval of the orthodox, decided to ingratiate himself once more with pious Muslims. Under this stimulus he wrote a poem *Yúsuf and Zulaykhá* in the *maṣnawí* form (i.e. rhyming in couplets). Yúsuf (Joseph) is in the Orient the ideal of manly perfection and beauty, and the story of his relationship with Zulaykhá, Potiphar's wife, is a favourite one. The author, in the preface to the work, says that he has in the past sung the legendary deeds of ancient princes, but that now, in his old age, he tunes his verse to a truer theme. Like the *Sháh-náma*, the work was followed by many efforts of the same kind, notably that of Jámí, but its literary worth is less than that of the epic poem, even though its orthodoxy was more acceptable to the faithful.

Amongst the scientists and historians that graced Maḥmúd's court was the renowned chronologist al Bírúní, who wrote in Arabic many works of importance, the chief being the *Áṣáru'l Báḳiya*, or 'Surviving Monuments', and the *Ta'ríkhu 'l Hind*, or 'History of India'. Maḥmúd also wished to seat at his 'Round Table', by force if need be, the incomparable physician and philosopher Avicenna (Abú 'Alí ibn Síná), whose fame had reached him; but the latter fled before Maḥmúd's agents, and took refuge at the court of the Ziyárid Prince Ḳábús ibn Washmgír, and finally at Rayy. He was a man of many parts who, besides being a master in medicine and philosophy, could write excellent *ḳaṣídas* in Arabic, and who probably composed many of the Persian quatrains afterwards attributed to 'Umar Khayyám as well as some *ghazals*. He also wrote in his native language a vast encyclopaedia of the sciences entitled *Dánish-náma i 'Alá'í*, or 'Book of Knowledge of 'Alá', 'Alá being the shortened form of 'Aláu 'l Dawla of Isfahán, for whom the work was compiled. His enormous reputation rests upon his Arabic prose works on medicine and philosophy. In these he interpreted and handed on the Greek tradition in a work which has been of enormous benefit to civilization. His 'Canon' not only dominated Islamic medicine for centuries—indeed, it is a standard text-book in Persia to this day—but was translated into Latin and, very soon after the invention of printing, became in Europe, too, one of the most often consulted works on the art of healing. His philosophy is embodied in his work the *Shifá*, which deals with physics, metaphysics, &c., and is a system of Aristotelianism mingled with native Persian pessimism and mysticism, which accorded well with the spirit abroad in Persia in his time, and gave him enduring popularity. He died in 1037 and was buried at Hamadán, where his tomb, which is still in existence, has become a place of pilgrimage for persons suffering from fevers and other ailments.

For verse of all kinds Persian usually held its own, but the prose of the time, except in Arabic, appears to have been scanty. The splendours of Maḥmúd's reign and the magnificence of his court were celebrated in Arabic prose by Maḥmúd's historian 'Utbí in his work *Ta'ríkhi Yamíní*, or 'The History of Yamínu 'l Dawla' ('the Right Hand of the State', one of Maḥmúd's many titles). The famous panegyrist Abú 'l Faẓl Aḥmad (d. A. D. 1008), generally known by the title of Badí'u 'l Zamán (Wonder of the Age) of Hamadán, is said to have composed a *ḳaṣída* in honour of Maḥmúd, but he is much better known as the inventor of *Maḳámát*, generally translated 'Séances', a form of Arabic composition in verse and rhymed prose which is the nearest approach to the dramatic form known in that language.

Maḥmúd had not the monopoly of literature in his day. As has been indicated, many of his panegyrists were bribed away or brought by force from other courts, of which Persia could boast at least half a dozen where were men of letters assured of a welcome. There seems to have been a constant movement of poets and scholars from court to court, the less successful changing patrons in the hope of greater reward, while princes competed for the more successful to add distinction to their establishments.

In the first half of the eleventh century A.D. the Saljúḳs, a family of Turkoman chieftains, yielding to pressure from the north, led their tribesmen into Persia, which, after some campaigning, they contrived to consolidate under their own rulership. Finding the nearest territory to them, the Ghaznawid kingdom, torn with internal dissension, they attacked and overthrew Maḥmúd's successor, thus confining the Ghaznawids henceforth to India with their capital at Lahore. Then, marching west and south, the Turkoman tribesmen overran the loosely-knit empire of the Buwayhids and entered Baghdad, where, under their chief Tughril Beg, they assumed the place of power in the Caliphate which had been held for so long by the Buwayhids.

Tughril Beg was succeeded by his nephew Alp Arslán and the latter by his son Malikshááh. The empire of these chieftains was enormous, stretching from Afghanistan to the borders of Egypt. Almost as a matter of course they gave their patronage to the men of letters that came to their court, for the matter of their own aggrandisement was never left to chance. One of the foremost literary men of their day was their own vizier 'Abú 'Alí al Ḥasan, generally known by his title of 'Niẓámu 'l Mulk'. He was born at Ṭús in Khurásán, into the family of a not too prosperous 'dihḳán' or village landowner, and after a time became vizier to Alp Arslán. In this capacity he played a great rôle. In addition to fulfilling his onerous duties of state he was able to encourage learning by the foundation of the famous college at Baghdad, called after him the 'Niẓámiya'. He also had some skill in literary composition and wrote a 'Treatise on the Art of Government' (*Siyásat-náma*), which is a manual of the principles of rulership based on the results of its author's interpretation of history and on his own experiences. Amongst the most interesting of its chapters are those which describe the growth of factions and separatist societies harmful to the commonwealth and destructive of right government. Of these he enumerates the Isma'ílís (of whom the Assassins were a branch), the Carmathians, Mazdakites, and others. His treatment of the subject of the Assassins is of interest, for, according to common report, he met his death at their hands in A.D. 1092.

The confederacy of the Isma'ílís here mentioned claims attention, but as being the subject of much writing rather than author of it. Their sect was originally a division of the Shí'a. Like the rest of the Shí'a they believed in a series of Imáms, divinely appointed religious leaders and successors of the Prophet, descended on the one side from Muḥammad, and on the other from the native Sasanian kings of Persia. The last of the Imáms, the so-called Mahdí, is hidden, and will one day reappear to become the prophet of the future. The Isma'ílís differ from the official Shí'a in acknowledging seven Imáms, of whom the seventh was called Isma'íl and gave his name to the movement, whereas the Shí'a claim the existence of twelve. In addition to this fundamental doctrine the Isma'ílís developed a mystical system in which emanation and incarnation played a large part, and in which the number seven was endowed with peculiar significance. The movement, in spite of its apparent concern with theological minutiae, was political rather than religious in effect, though as a general rule it is difficult in Islam to distinguish between the two. The remarkable methods of propaganda instituted by the first 'Grand Master' of the sect, the notorious Ḥasan i Sabbáḥ, gained them many proselytes from the whole of the Near East. One of these methods was the use of 'ḥashísh', which is a drug extracted from hemp and which has given rise to the name 'Assassin', a corruption of *ḥashíshí* ('hemp-eater'), with its evil significance. In

Syria the Isma'ílís gained a hideous reputation for their activities during the Crusades, as a result of which the name of their chief, which the Crusaders introduced into Europe as 'The Old Man of the Mountains', remained for centuries a source of terror.

Intimately connected with the history of the Isma'ílís was the life-story of the philosopher and traveller Náṣiri Khusraw (A.D. 1004–88). His life and work seem to have been conditioned by constant speculation on the origin and fate of man and the world. Persistent search for a solution to his problems led him to the study of all branches of knowledge and into many foreign lands. His '*Safar-náma*' or 'Diary' of his journey, gives a long account of what he had seen and done in Persia, Syria, Palestine, Arabia, Egypt, and elsewhere. As a contemporary record of the social and political conditions in those countries the work is of immense value besides being of considerable topographical interest. It appears to have been written from the Sunní point of view, and the author almost certainly commenced his travels as a Sunní. At Cairo, however, which was then the seat of the (Shí'a) Fáṭimid Caliphate, he was converted to Shí'ism, and finally attached himself to the Isma'ílís. In their cause he worked zealously, and, though he took no part in their political development, he helped them greatly in the diffusion of their ideas. To those that know the Baṣra of to-day and the great camp that existed during the late war at Ma'ḳil (which to the British Army was known as *Margil*), Náṣir's description of Baṣra as he saw it, and of an adventure there, will be of interest:

On the 24th of Sha'bán 443 [A. H., = 28th December A. D. 105] we reached the town of Baṣra. It has a great wall except on the side near the river. The latter is that known as the 'Shaṭṭ', which is the Tigris and Euphrates that join at the extreme boundary of the Baṣra administrative district. Those streams, with the confluent river of

Jubára they call the 'Shaṭṭu 'l 'Arab'. Two great canals take off from this river, the distance between their inlets being one parasang. They have been directed towards the Ḳibla [i.e. south-west] and after flowing for four parasangs they join and flow together southward for a parasang. From these canals numberless small canals derive and lead in all directions, and on their banks date groves and orchards have been planted. Of these two canals, the upper one, to the north-east, is called the Ma'ḳil canal, and that to the south-west the Ubulla canal. Between the two canals a large island has arisen in the shape of an elongated rectangle, at the narrow end of which lies Baṣra. Everywhere to the south and west of Baṣra is a desert without cultivation, water, or trees. . . .

The markets were held daily at Baṣra in three places; in the morning at the place called 'Suḳu 'l Khazá'a' ('Camel-meat Bazaar'), at mid-day in the place called 'Súḳ 'Uṣmán' (''Uṣmán's Bazaar'), and at the end of the day in the place they call 'Súḳu 'l Ḳaddáhín' (the 'Potter's Bazaar'). Business was transacted in the following manner: any one that had goods of value delivered them to a money-changer, and received from him a receipt. If he needed anything he purchased it, and referred [the seller] to the money-changer for payment. While they remained in the city, people paid in nothing but money-changer's notes.

When we reached Baṣra, our state of nakedness and misery was such that we were like madmen. It was three months since we had last untied our hair, and I wished to go to the warm-baths in the hope of getting warm, for the weather was cold and we had no clothes, I and my brother being clad in an old loin-cloth with a torn sack tied on our backs against the cold. I thought, 'Who will let us into his bath now?' Thereupon I sold a small saddle-bag in which I had kept my books, and out of the proceeds I put a few coppers into a piece of paper to give to the bathman that I might he allowed to remain in the bath a little longer and rid myself of dirt. But when I placed the miserable coppers in front of him he looked at us, and taking us for lunatics told us to be off, for the people were then leaving the baths; and he would not let us enter. In shame we emerged and hastily departed.

The results of Náṣir's philosophical speculations are given in the works subsequent to his *Safar-náma*, namely, the *Díwán*, the *Rawshaná'i-náma*, the *Sa'ádat-náma*, and the *Zádu 'l Musáfirín*. The poems collected in the *Díwán* deal mainly with the author's religious tenets, and are often coloured by Isma'ílí ideas, while the *Rawshaná'i-náma* (Book of Enlightenment) and the *Sa'ádat-náma* are two *maṣnawí* poems which illustrate the development of the poet's views of life. Both contain bitter attacks on the hypocrisy, vanity, and folly of earthly life, the *Sa'ádat-nama* devoting itself in particular to denouncing the short-comings of princes. The *Zádu 'l Musáfirín* (Viaticum) is a detailed exposition of the author's religious and philosophical foundations for his beliefs. From the blend of the practical with the mystical which Náṣir employs in his poetry, he may be looked upon as one of the earliest of the didactics, and his methods foreshadow those adopted in the purely didactic works which afterwards became frequent.

This is well brought out in the following section from the *Rawshaná'i-náma*.

Know thyself, for knowing truly thine own heart
Thou knowest what good and ill in thee have part.
Discern the worth of thine own being, and then
Walk with pride amidst the common run of men.
Know thyself, and the whole world thus discover,
Then from all ill shalt thou thyself deliver.
Thou knowest not thyself for thou art lowly,
Thou shouldst behold God if thou thyself couldst see.
Nine spheres and seven stars for thee do service,
Thou art, alas, to thine own body 'prentice.
Go cast away from thee all pleasures carnal—
If thou in truth dost seek delight eternal.
Be a man! Care nought for viands or for sleep;
In thyself, like wand'ring monk, go, journey deep.
For viands and sleep solely concern the brutes,
Whereas thy soul in thought and spirit hath its roots.
Arouse thyself! How long more wilt thou slumber?
See thyself, full of marvels without number.
Consider well, have regard whence comest thou;
In this prison for what cause lingerest thou?
Break thy cage and flight to thine own stronghold take;
Dare like Abraham thine images to break.
As now thou art, for a purpose wast thou made,
Alas, if to perform it thou hast delayed.
Woe when an angel is Satan's servitor,
Woe when a king is slave to his janitor.
How comes it that Jesus is bereft of sight,
When in one eye's vision Korah may delight?
There is a dragon keeps the treasure from thee;
The monster slay, and of all dull care be free.
Coward thou art if on thy nurture he thrive,
Then of boundless wealth canst thou no share derive.
A beggar thou art, though thine house hold the store;
The balm is to thine hand, yet stay'st thou heart-sore.

Thou sleepest! Into what lodging art thou brought
With charm bedight, yet for the hoard without thought!
Quick, break the chain, bear away that treasure rare;
Have one care only, and that—to cast out care.

Of far greater spiritual influence and literary importance than the Isma'ílí doctrines was Ṣúfíism, a system of theosophic mysticism which began to gain converts in Persia soon after the Islamic conquest. Its origin is a matter of debate. Partly it seems to have been the outcome of Aryan revolt against the absolute rigidity of Islam—and yet its earliest exponents were themselves Arabs and ascetics who wore rough garments of wool (Arabic *ṣúf*), which gave the movement its name. Partly it was the result of greater freedom of speculation which was produced when Persia came into its own again under the 'Abbásid Caliphs. There are traces in the movement of neo-Platonist ideas, and some scholars have seen the marks in it of Indian influences. Mysticism was certainly not the exclusive property of Persia; it was common to most lands in the Middle Ages when men were seeking for some means of piercing the veil of the unknown in order to find the formula for achieving the well-being of their souls, just as they sought an explanation of the physical world in the pursuit of the philosopher's stone.

In Persia it had somehow to be reconciled with Islam. His belief in God helped the Muslim to absorb Ṣúfíism, for the foundation of Ṣúfíism is that God is the only reality, also that He is 'Truth' itself. Besides that, there exists a bond of mystical love between God and man, and, since God is the only reality, every man must be or have within him a portion of the Godhead separated from its source and for ever striving after reunion. Ecstasy achieves the desired object for a moment, but 'permanence' in union can only be acquired by 'annihilation' of the flesh, which is the veil and the barrier. The elimination of the flesh and the attainment of permanent union can be brought about by travel along a certain 'Path', the stages of which were differently defined by the various 'Pírs' or Ṣúfí spiritual leaders. The doctrine of God's identity with man and the world led inevitably to pantheism, and to scepticism concerning the doctrines of orthodox Islam. Its logical product was such a man as Manṣúri Ḥalláj, an early Ṣúfí who suffered death for his dictum, 'I am the Truth', i.e. God.

An extract from the prologue to the *Maṣnawí i Ma'nawí* (The Spiritual Maṣnawí) of Jalálu 'l Dín Rúmí, will illustrate how Ṣúfíism presented itself to the poet:

Hail to thee, O love, our sweet melancholy.
Thou physician of all our ills;
Thou purge of our pride and conceit,
That art our Plato and our Galen.
Our earthy body, through love, is raised to the skies,
Mountains take to dancing and to nimbleness.
Love became the soul of Sinai, lover!
Sinai was intoxicated 'and Moses fell swooning'.
Its secret is hidden 'twixt topmost treble and lowest bass,
Were I to reveal it I'd shatter the world.
But, were I close to my confidant's lips,
I would, like the reed-pipe, say all my say.
He that is far from men that speak his tongue
Is speechless, though he have a hundred voices.
When the rose is gone and the rose-garden passed away,
Thou wilt no more hear the bulbul's song.
When the rose is gone and the rose-garden fallen to ruin,
Whence wilt thou seek the rose's scent? From rose-water?
The All is the belovèd and the lover a veil;
The living is the belovèd and the lover a thing dead.
When love no more has His attraction,
It remains like a bird without power of flight.

. . . .

What can I say? My thoughts move preposterously
If I have not the light of my Friend before and behind.

. . . .

Knowest thou why thy mirror will not reflect [love]?
Because the rust [of sin] is not cleansed from its face.

The importance of Ṣúfíism in Persian literature comes from the fact that it imbued practically the whole of Persian poetry with its spirit. With the notable exception of Firdawsí the greater poets all gave expression to its mysticism and ideals; but most of the lyricists, it is true, merely employed the metaphors and figures of the system to add beauty to their compositions; but most of the great poets treated Ṣúfiism itself as their first concern, and it is to poetry thereby inspired that one must look to find the esoteric meaning of the system. The prose works on Ṣúfiism merely analyse it without revealing its spirit.

The first poet of note in the Ṣúfí movement was Abú Sa'íd ibn Abí 'l Khayr (A.D. 968–1049), who revived and popularized the quatrain as a verse form and established its position as a common vehicle of mystical thought. He also laid the foundation of that system of metaphors and symbols familiar in the work of his successors, which uses the language of earthly and bodily pleasure to describe Divine Love and which, for lack of a better, has been employed to a greater or less extent by all believers in the love of a Divine Being. Its limitations are seen in Rabbinical and early Christian literature, which abounds in curiously anthropomorphic pictures of the Godhead; but nowhere does symbolism take such strange forms as in Ṣúfí poetry, where love, wine, and beauty are all brought into service to picture the relationships between God and man.

Later than Abú Sa'íd, and contemporary with Náṣiri Khusraw, was the mystic Anṣárí of Harát, who displayed in his themes, both in prose and verse, the same mixture of practical ethics and theosophy that was visible in some of Náṣir's work. He is best known for his quatrains and for his *Munáját*, which are prayers or addresses to God, interspersed with exhortations and advice to fellow Ṣúfís.

Another Ṣúfí pioneer was Saná'í, who began his career as a court poet at Ghazna, and who was the first to employ the *maṣnawí* form as a mode of Ṣúfí expression. His work is not always purely mystical, but sometimes has in addition practical and didactic aims. The *Ḥadíḳatu 'l Ḥaḳíḳa* (The Garden of Truth) is his best known *maṣnawí*. It is often called the forerunner of the *Manṭiḳu 'l Ṭayr*, the great allegorical poem of Farídu 'l Dín 'Aṭṭár, and also of the mystical *maṣnawí* of Jalálu 'l Dín Rúmí. The *Hadiḳa* is made up of ten sections of very mixed content, dealing with the Unity of God, Reason, Knowledge, Philosophy, the Futility of Earthly Life, and Mystical Love, but the treatment is poor and the illustrative anecdotes frequently fail in their effect. Of much greater worth, though less well known, are the lyrical poems included in the author's *díwán*. The basic mystical theme of the soul's sojourn on earth is employed in the following *ghazal*:

> Some few days in this world I did remain,
> And over earth's surface traversed the wind.
> I wandered much, and much I saw of pain,
> Though not a night to lust was I inclined.
> In wrath no man was harmed by my satires;
> From me none gained praise mean and undeserved:
> From evil lusts and sensual desires
> My pure soul I immaculate preserved.
> In those days when my spirit was at ease
> Upon mine inwardness no grief had grown;
> And when time came for Fate on me to seize
> I reaped the harvest from the seed I'd sown.
> My soul to its essence again had won;
> I was freed from pain, peace had come to me.
> Whither I had wandered was known to none,
> And where I'd roamed to me is mystery.

Alongside the ecstatic spiritualism of the Ṣúfís lies the colder pessimistic scepticism of 'Umar Khayyám, who therein followed in the footsteps of Avicenna. 'Umar ibn Ibrahím al Khayyám, ('Umar son of Ibrahím the Tent-maker) of Níshápúr is better known in his own country as an astronomer, mathematician, and free-thinker than as a poet. He was certainly no professional panegyrist, for there is not a line of mercenary flattery in any of his work; but whether his own countrymen's estimate of him as a poet be just or not—and native opinion often differs from that of foreign critics—it is in his poetry that he is most typically Persian. In it he shows himself the chief and foremost of that group of free-thinkers who satirized the narrowness of dogma and taught the futility of piety and virtue. They regarded God as responsible for all the sorrows of mankind, and preached that blind fate rather than any Divine Providence ruled the world. Even pleasure, which, according to 'Umar, is the only *raison d'être* for life, leads nowhere and is vanity of vanities. It is not to be wondered at that 'Umar's philosophy was not always to the taste of pious Muslims and that he was subjected to much persecution.

It is of course a generally known fact now that the quatrains which Fitzgerald wove into the exquisite poem that has achieved such popularity in the West, are in reality a series of disconnected epigrams, of which some at least may be the work of other poets. If it may be assumed that the majority of the verses were the work of 'Umar they seem to have been composed at various periods of his life, and the contradictions in them are to be explained by the progress of his ideas as he passed through all the stages from pious Muslim to avowed sceptic. His sole consistency lies in his praise of wine, to which in his hopelessness he turns for oblivion and perhaps for exaltation.

Of 'Umar's scientific work, a treatise in Arabic on Algebra and another on some definitions of Euclid are known. He is also credited with part authorship of certain astronomical tables, the *Zíj i Malikshâhí* (the Malikshah Tables), the name of which makes it appear more than probable that at some period 'Umar came into contact with Malikshâh's vizier, the Niẓámu 'l Mulk. The well-known story, however, that 'Umar went to school with the Niẓámu 'l Mulk and with the Isma'ílí Grand Master of Assassins, Ḥasani Sabbáḥ, has been discredited on chronological grounds.

His death date is generally given as A.D. 1123, though there is no certain evidence for it.

Mystic poetry by no means represented the total sum of literary energy during the political domination of the Saljúḳs. The writing of romances based on Iranian materials had not ceased entirely. There is at least one surviving specimen by al Jurjání, who lived under Tughril Beg. This work is the historical romance of *Wís and Rámín* (composed about A.D. 1048) which has been compared for its treatment and the psychological truth of its *dénouement* with the German romance of *Tristan und Isolde.*

Persian prose was still comparatively rare as a medium of expression, though it was used for encyclopaedias of science and the like. A notable example of such early scientific work was the *Ẕakhíra'i Khwárazmsháhí* or 'Khwárazmsháhí Thesaurus', which is a large medical textbook compiled in the second decade of the twelfth century by Zaynu 'l Dín al Jurjání and dedicated by him to the founder of the Khwárazm dynasty. About the time when the *Siyásat-náma* of the Niẓámu 'l Mulk was being written, another somewhat similar work was undertaken by Káy Káus ibn Iskandar, the grandson of the Ziyárid prince Ḳábús, in whose honour it was called the *Ḳábús-náma.* It was a manual of ethics for princes, the author's immediate object in writing it being to guide his son through the intricacies of government and the difficulties of kingship. The book is written in the strain of practical wisdom associated in Persia with the names of the legendary personages Húshang, Jamshíd, and Luḳmán, and often too with the name of Núshírwán the Just, who is regarded as the Solomon of his country. Their wise sayings provide the moralists with ever popular pegs upon which to hang their discourses, the resultant writings being numerous enough to form a Persian 'Wisdom Literature', though it never reaches the high plane of the Book of Job, or even that of Proverbs.

An epoch in the development of the Faith of Islam and Ṣúfíism was marked by the famous mystical divine and moralist al Ghazálí († A.D. 1111). His work belongs rather to Arabic than to Persian literature, but he was himself a Persian born at Ṭús and a client of the Niẓámu 'l Mulk. Though he wrote for the most part in Arabic, he summarized in Persian, under the title of *Kímíyá i Sa'ádat* (The Alchemy of Felicity), his most important book *Iḥyá 'Ulúmu 'l Dín* (Revival of the Sciences of the Faith). It is a general work on theology and a compendium of Muḥammadanism, written with a Ṣúfí bias that foreshadows the author's ultimate absorption into Ṣúfíism. To Ghazálí more than to other doctors is due the credit for analysing, formulating, and classifying the teachings which the Ṣúfí poets decorate and illumine in the imagery of their verses. In spite of this, his services to Islamic orthodoxy were so great that the title *Ḥujjatu 'l Islám* (The Proof of Islam) was bestowed upon him.

Another aspect of the literary activity of the time was displayed by the translation of the fables of Bidpai, or Pilpai, from Arabic into Persian by Naṣru 'lláh ibnu 'l Ḥamíd who dedicated it to the Ghaznawid Sultan Bahrámsháh (A.D. 1118–52). The translation was made in prose from Ibnu 'l Muḳaffa''s Arabic version of the book, which was originally a series of Buddhist tales written in Sanskrit. In the sixth century of our era it had been translated into Pahlawi and thence into Arabic, from which several Persian versions were made. Of these, the first was Rúdagí's *maṣnawí* translation, but of this no trace has remained; then came Naṣru 'lláh's translation, which was followed in the sixteenth century by the most widely known—though not the best—version of all, the *Anwári Suhaylí* of Ḥusayn Wá'iẓ Káshifí.

The middle Saljúḳ period boasts the *Chahár Maḳála*

(Four Discourses) of Niẓámí i 'Arúẓí i Samarḳandí. The author was a court poet in the service of the kings of Ghúr in Transoxiana for forty-five years, and there he wrote the work by which he is best known and on which alone in fact, his reputation is based. The *Chahár Maḳála* is a biographical, quasi-philosophical composition, interspersed with many poetical quotations, and consists of an introduction and four discourses:—on the secretarial function, on the art of poetry, on astrology, and on medicine. Each is illustrated by numerous anecdotes concerning persons whom the author had met, and places which he had visited in the course of his travels, many of them of great biographical value, since they furnish materials earlier in date than those ordinarily quoted by the biographers and bibliographers. The panegyrist's professional touch is added in the introduction which dedicates the work, with the usual rhetorical flourishes, to Abú 'l Ḥasan 'Alí ibn Mas'úd, a prince of the Ghúrid House and the author's patron. The opening paragraphs of this preface provide an excellent specimen of the general run of these compositions, and they are here given in the translation of Professor Browne[1]:

Praise and thanks and glory to that King who, by the instrumentality of the Cherubim and Angels of the Spirit world, brought into being the World of Return and Restoration, and, by means thereof, created and adorned the World of Becoming and Decay, maintaining it by the Command and Prohibition of the Prophets and Saints, and restraining it by the swords and pens of Kings and Ministers. And blessings upon the Lord of both worlds, who was the most perfect of the Prophets, and invocations of grace upon his Companions and those of his Household, who were the most excellent of Saints and Vicars. And honour to the King of this time, that learned, just, divinely-favoured, victorious, and heaven-aided monarch *Husamu 'd-Dawla wa 'd-Dín*, Helper of Islam and the Muslims, Exterminator of the infidels and polytheists, Subduer of the heretical and the froward, Supporter of hosts in the worlds, Pride of Kings and Emperors, Succourer of mankind, Protector of these days, Fore-arm of the Caliphate, Beauty of the Faith and Glory of the Nation, Order of the Arabs and the Persians, noblest of mankind, *Shamsu 'l-Ma'ali, Maliku 'l-Umará*, Abu 'l-Hasan 'Alí b. Mas'úd, Help

[1] From the Journal of the Royal Asiatic Society, 1899, p. 619 f.

of the Prince of Believers, may his life be filled with success, may the greater part of the world be assigned to his name, and may the ordering of the affairs of Adam's seed be directed by his care. For to-day he is the most excellent of the kings of the age in nobility, pedigree, doughty deeds, judgement, statesmanship, justice, equality, valour, and generosity, as well as in the adorning of his territory, the embellishment of his realms, the maintenance of his friends, the subjugation of his foes, the raising of armies, the safeguarding of the people, the securing of the roads, and the tranquillizing of the realms, and also in that upright judgement, clear understanding, strong resolve, and firm determination, by the excellence of which the concatenation of the House of Shansab is held together and maintained in order, and by the perfection of which the strong arm of that Dynasty is strengthened and braced. May God Almighty give him full portion, together with the other kings of that line, of dominion and domain, and throne and fortune, by His Favour and His Grace!

The group of panegyrists and *ḳaṣída* writers of the Saljúḳ period, with Anwarí at the head, are considered in Persia to be the best of their kind. Anwarí, the favourite eulogist of Maliksháh's grandson, the Sultan Sanjar of Khurásán (1117–57), is held by native critics to be not only the best writer of *ḳaṣídas* but one of the ablest poets in Persia. But though it is true that his power of expression and the beauty of his diction entitle him to consideration as a poet, yet his *ḳaṣídas* make dull and difficult reading even to a Persian. The reason is that they are expressly designed to flatter some particular patron and are, moreover, weighted with hyperbole and filled with far-fetched similes and obsure references to Oriental custom and Islamic ritual that constantly demand explanation. To some extent the sum of flattery is relieved by discreetly impersonal satire, but this does not make Anwarí's *ḳaṣídas* palatable to Western tastes. His elegies are in a different category, for they contain elements that can be more generally appreciated. A particularly graphic example is that which has often been translated under the title of *The Tears of Khurásán*, a lament for the destruction of Khurásán by the Turkoman tribe of the Ghuzz about the year A.D. 1154.

The spirited but somewhat free version made by Captain William Kirkpatrick and published in the Asiatick Miscellany (Calcutta 1785), contains the following verses which will give some idea of the poem :—

X

Ah! with benignity incline thine ear,
A piteous tale of misery to hear,
  Nor to our woes the starting tear deny:
But as the dismal sounds shall pierce thy soul,
Oh yield thee to compassion's soft control,
  And as she prompts, quick to our succour fly.

XI

Thee, thus great champion of our sacred law,
Whose virtue and whose zeal inspire with awe,
  Whom vice or frailty to sin provoke:
Thee thus Irania's groaning sons address,
Whom inward fires consume, and foes oppress.

XII

Say dost thou know what wild confusion reigns
Throughout Irania's desolated plains,
  And how her sons are drown'd in seas of tears?
Say dost thou know, of all her ancient boast,
And glorious sights that spread her fame the most,
  No trace or mournful vestige now appears?

Almost as famous a poet as Anwarí in his own country is the panegyrist Kháḳání, who spent the greater part of his life in the compilation of eulogies on princes of his native province of Shírwán. The intricate word plays and pedantic allusions with which his *ḳaṣídas* abound makes them even more obscure than those of Anwarí. Amongst his other works, some of which make easier reading, is the *maṣnawí* poem *Tuḥfatu 'l 'Iráḳayn* (Gift of the Two Iráḳs). He composed it whilst on a pilgrimage to Mecca and describes the two Iráḳs (Persian Iráḳ and Arab Iráḳ), through which he passed on his journey. On his return home he appears to have offended his patron, it is said, by an indiscreet display of spiritual pride, and was thrown into prison. His incarceration, however, was not without its literary advantages, for it provided him with materials for his *Ḥabsíya*, or 'Prison Poem', to which Oscar Wilde's *Ballad of Reading Gaol* bears at least outward resemblance. In the extract here given some attempt is made to preserve the monorhyme proper to the *ḳaṣída*:

As on my iron couch I lay my trembling limbs,
  Heaven itself 's atremble at my grievous sigh.
I kiss my chain; ah me, for it gives me counsel;
  Though my bonds upon my neck as a kerchief lie,
Bound in darkest sorrow I show the face of morn,
  And my dwelling black as night gleams white to mine eye.
My back 's to the prison wall, my face to heaven,
  Tears fill my eyes, many as stars that fill the sky.
Grief and I come face to face as kernel and shell,
  In cell close-roofed with woe unbroken, there dwell I.
Each day my grievous sighing rises unto God.
  How long shall all my nights be filled with my sore cry?
Clear it is as morn that with each morning's rising
  Comes resurrection, and I from foul night can fly.

Panegyric verse seems to fill an unduly large place in the literary history of the time. This was due to the fact that every Persian court encouraged versifiers to compose in return for the crumbs from the patrons' tables. The poetry produced under this stimulus may conform to Jámí's definition of poetry as verbal fancies in rhyme and metre. It is certainly not a criticism of life. For that one must go to the mystics or the lyric poets. But the panegyrists occasionally give glimpses into the times in which they lived, and thereby provide any value they have for the general reader. Many of the lesser poets contemporary with Anwarí, were able to produce occasional work whose merit was not wholly ephemeral. Thus Aṣíru 'l Dín Akhsíkatí wrote *ḳaṣídas* of which some are considered by Persians to be as good as those of Anwarí himself; Amír Mu'izzí (1147–8), Sanjar's poet laureate, left a *díwán* which contains some interesting mystical elements; Rashídi Waṭwáṭ is chiefly known for an excellent treatise on Persian prosody, the *Ḥadáiḳu 'l Siḥr* (Gardens of Enchantment);

and even Súzaní († 1173–4) the satirist who, according to Jámí, had a frivolous disposition and was much given to levity, set a fashion by his biting sarcasms and gibing caricatures of the serious-minded versifiers of his day. The biographers say that he repented before his death, became a pupil of the mystic Saná'í, and wrote *ḳaṣídas* in praise of the Imáms, but it is his parodies that made most mark in Persian literature.

A poet of the period who had some degree of fame amongst his contemporaries was Adíb Ṣábir of Tirmíz, to whom Anwarí once likened himself with some pride. After serving for a time at the court of the governor of Khurásán at Níshápúr he was able, on the strength of his skill in versification, to gain entrance into Sultán Sanjar's entourage. He must then have impressed that monarch by his ability, for when Sanjar's vassal, the Khwárazmsháh Atsiz, rebelled against the authority of the Sultán, Adíb was sent to Khwárazm by the latter on a mission either of conciliation or espionage. In any case, to judge from the poet's extant *ḳaṣídas*, he appears to have been not unfavourably received. His end, however, was tragic. Having discovered a plot for the assassination of Sanjar by an agent of Atsiz, he reported it to his master without taking sufficient precaution to keep his action hidden from the Khwárazmian. The latter in revenge had the poet drowned in the Oxus. The date of this last event is variously placed by the biographers between A.D. 1143 and 1152.

The power to inspire which the ancient Iranian legends had possessed for Firdawsí was still strong in Saljúḳ days. Romantic poetry, based upon the stories of famous lovers taken from the legends, found a pioneer in Niẓámí of Ganja (the modern Elizabetpol). His themes concern themselves with the erotic rather than with the warlike adventures of the ancient heroes, and though ancient legend provided the materials for his compositions, they are more fittingly called romances than epics. Niẓámí was born at Ḳum, probably in A.D. 1141, and was brought up in rigid Sunní surroundings that seem for a time to have obscured his poetic faculties. He did not produce his first work, the *Makhzanu 'l Asrár*, or 'Treasure-house of Secrets', until he was forty years of age. The book, which was a collection of ethical and religious maxims in the *maṣnawí* form, was deeply coloured by the author's upbringing, though the style of many illustrative anecdotes in it foreshadowed the wealth of diction and descriptive power that characterized the romances which succeeded it. In the later works, psychological truth and effectiveness of imagery and description reach a high standard; and even if it is true that the poet cannot forgo an occasional hint of the superiority of Islam over the paganism of his heroes, yet such incidental propaganda is rare and is outweighed by the sincerity and elegance of diction and by the vividness of description with which his work is filled. His literary qualities fully justify his being called the second great classical poet of Persia.

His first romance, *Khusraw u Shírín*, was composed a year or two after the *Makhzanu 'l Asrár*. It deals with the story of the Sasanian prince Khusraw Parwíz and his love for the Armenian princess Shírín. The 'knot' in the story is provided by the princess's love for a third character, the master-builder Farhád, who meets a tragic end. *Khusraw u Shírín* was followed by *Laylá u Majnún*, the scene of which is laid in the Arabian desert. The story is the familiar one of lovers that belong to families bitterly at enmity with one another and so determined in their opposition to the wedding that the lovers only find union in death. The material for Niẓámí's fourth *maṣnawí* was provided by the life of the Sasanian king, Bahrám Gúr. The *Haft Paykar*, or 'Seven Effigies', as it is called, is a collection of seven stories, each told to the king by one of his seven favourite wives, somewhat after the style of the *Arabian Nights*. The last of the poet's *maṣnawís*, the *Iskandar-náma* (Book of Alexander), has for its theme the life of Alexander. The subject is treated in pure epic style, but with a mystical touch which makes Alexander a prophet as well as a conqueror. The five poems are traditionally grouped under the heading of *Khamsa* (Quintet), or *Panj Ganj* (Five Treasures), and they have provided a model that has found an enormous number of copiers. The poet died soon after the completion of his last poem, probably in A. D. 1203.

The exaggerated sweetness and pathos of Niẓámí's work, though they suit the native taste admirably, are yet somewhat trying to those brought up in a different literary atmosphere. For that reason, possibly, his poems have not been so often translated into English as their popularity in Persia would lead one to expect. A translation of *Laylá and Majnún*, published in 1836 and reprinted in 1894, was made by James Atkinson, from whose version is taken the following description of the hero's emotions after his meeting with Laylá:

By worldly prudence uncontrolled,
Their every glance their feelings told;
For true lover never yet had skill
To veil impassioned looks at will.
When ringlets of a thousand curls,
And ruby lips, and teeth of pearls,
And dark eyes flashing quick and bright,
Like lightning on the brow of night—
When charms like these their power display,
And steal the withered heart away—
Can man, dissembling, coldly seem
Unmoved as by an idle dream?
Kais [Majnún] saw her beauty, saw her grace,
The soft expression of her face;
And as he gazed, and gazed again,
Distraction stung his burning brain:
No rest he found by day or night—
Lailí for ever in his sight.

But, oh! when separation came,
More brightly glowed his ardent flame;
And she, with equal sorrow fraught,
Bewailed the fate upon them brought.
—He wandered wild through lane and street,
With frantic step, as if to meet
Something, which still his search defied,
Reckless of all that might betide.
His bosom heaved with groans and sighs,
Tears ever gushing from his eyes;
And still he struggled to conceal
The anguish he was doomed to feel;
And, maddened with excessive grief,
In the lone desert sought relief.
Thither as morning dawned, he flew;
His head and feet no covering knew;
And every night, with growing pain,
The woes of absence marked his strain.
The secret path he eager chose
Where Lailí's distant mansion rose;
And kissed the door, and in that kiss
Fancied he quaffed the cup of bliss.
How fleet his steps to that sweet place!
A thousand wings increased his pace;
But thence, his fond devotions paid,
A thousand thorns his course delayed.

The Ṣúfí tradition in poetry was carried on after Saná'í by the infinitely abler poet and allegorist Farídu 'l Dín 'Aṭṭár (fl. A.D. 1119–1230?) His pen-name ''Aṭṭár' indicates the poet's original calling, that of a druggist, which he followed until his convictions led him to join the Ṣúfís, who had in his day become a regular order of wandering dervishes. His travels brought him into contact with most of the leading men of his way of thinking, and in the course of a very long life—if the tradition is true that he was put to death during the sack of Níshápúr by Chingiz Khán in A.D. 1230—he managed to assimilate much of the Ṣúfís' lore and to contribute ideas of his own. The result is a somewhat prosaic but elaborately worked out scheme of mystical doctrine set out in a great array of compositions. 'Aṭṭár's chief new contribution was an increase in the 'Stages' on the Ṣúfí 'Path' from three to seven. They are described in the *Manṭiḳu 'l Ṭayr* (Speech of the Birds), an allegorical *maṣnawí* describing with splendid imagery the adventures of the birds (i.e. the Ṣúfís), who travel through seven wonderful valleys (the seven stages) in search of their king, the Símurgh or Phoenix (i.e. the Truth). The tribulations of the birds and their varying fortunes represent the trials undergone by the seekers after Truth, and the account of them gives the work a general resemblance to Bunyan's *Pilgrim's Progress.*

In the thirty-eighth *maḳála* or discourse in the book, the hoopoe, who is elected the leader of the birds, in reply to a question from one of them, outlines the course of the pilgrimage as in the prose translation here given:

Another said to him: 'O, thou that knowest the path, our eyes are obscured in this desert,

The way appears full of terror, O, thou that art our friend, how many parasangs are there on this road?'

He replied: 'We must traverse seven valleys on the way. When the seven are past then comes the palace (of the Símurgh).

From this journey none returns to the world and none knoweth the number of its parasangs.

Since none cometh back from this far journey, how canst thou be informed, O thou of little patience?

Since all are utterly lost there, how can news be brought to thee, fool that thou art?

The valley of "Seeking" is the beginning of our labours, thereafter comes the boundless valley of "Love".

Third is the valley of "Knowledge", and fourth the valley of "All-Sufficiency".

Then is the fifth valley of pure "One-ness",—and sixth, the arduous valley of "Amazement".

The seventh valley is "Poverty" and "Annihilation", beyond which thou canst go no farther.

Thou wilt fall under some attractive force and thy power of movement will be lost; a drop will be to thee as an ocean.'

The *Manṭiḳu 'l Ṭayr* is the most widely known of 'Aṭṭár's works, but even more popular in Persia is a little book entitled the *Pand-náma* (Book of Advice). It is a compilation of platitudes of practical and ethical wisdom of the kind so beloved in the East, and so often a mainstay of conversation. Of much greater value is the author's *Tazkiratu 'l Awliyá* (Memoirs of the Saints), which provides a series of biographies of the early Ṣúfís, and contains much that is of interest for the study of the development of Ṣúfíism.

The works mentioned are amongst the larger of 'Aṭṭár's *maṣnawí* poems. Numerous lesser works which yet remain unpublished exist in manuscript form in the Bodleian Library and elsewhere. All of them are of mystical content treated in various fashions. *Gul u Hurmuz* (The Rose and Hurmuz) is a mystical romance, the *Muṣíbat-náma* (Book of Ill-fate) consists of a number of legends and fables, each designed to point a theosophic moral; the *Shutur-náma* (The Camel Book) describes the soul seeking after God under the simile of a camel bearing a pilgrim towards the sanctuary at Mecca, and the *Bulbul-náma* (The Nightingale Book) resembles the *Muṣíbat-náma* in being a series of edifying discourses illustrated by anecdotes and legends. A fable from the *Muṣíbat-náma* and another from the *Bulbul-náma* are given here in prose translations. The second bears obvious affinities with one of Aesop's fables.

THE FABLE OF THE POT AND THE GOBLET

There lived in the kitchen of Jamshíd (O wondrous story)
A pot and a goblet that quarrelled night and day.
The pot was of stone and determined on battle,
The goblet was of gold and ready for war.
Both in anger debated;
Stone and gold as they were they came to a trial of strength.
Said the pot to the goblet: 'Whether it be water or oil,
Salt or sweet, whatever it be, *I* contain it.
Where would your work be in the order of things without me?
If I did not supply you, you would remain empty for ever.
You first appeared out of stone,
Then you were pounded upon a stone to test you.
If you had no ballast in your constitution
You would fall constantly.
You are thus adorned and heavy through me.

You are endowed with dignity [lit. stone] and gravity through me.
Even though you keep on calling me a black pot,
You are miserly [lit. a black goblet] everywhere.
Have you never heard that agreeable saying?'
When these words fell on the senses of the goblet
His blood boiled like a pot.
Said he: 'You are what you contain, nor more nor less,
I stand empty before Jamshíd for what I am.
Arise and let us go to the goldsmith's
And discover which of us two is the better.
If the goldsmith possess a touch-stone,
That will reply to this boaṣting.'
In a wager faults are revealed,
At a time of wagering deeds are revealed.
Until you undertake a journey into yourself
How can you yourself ever come upon your sin?
If you find the way to your own sin it is well.
You will find that the angels derive from yourself,
But until you make the journey within,
This view will, in truth, never be yours.

THE FABLE OF THE TOWN MOUSE AND THE COUNTRY MOUSE

It is told in story that a rural mouse went with a town mouse for a walk in the country, and that they went in company to visit the country mouse. The country mouse dwelt in the wilderness. For his food he had grass seed, and rain for water. When the town mouse perceived this poverty, he said: 'But what is this? You have neither sweetstuff nor pleasant water nor bread. Is this how you live? Come to town and see my house, and in what manner my victuals are laid out.' With a hundred such tales he bore him off as a guest to his house and took him into the privacy of his own apartment, where he spread out two hundred kinds of varied wealth and sweetstuffs. But suddenly there came a cat like the splendour of Baghdad and put his head in at the door of the hole. Said the town mouse to the country mouse: 'This is a creditor of mine. I have borrowed gold from him. I am slow in amassing it.' [To the cat] 'Be so good as to return, brother, I have not the gold ready now.'

The country mouse approached and saw the cat, and outwardly he trembled and in his heart he was afraid. And the cat struck out his paw and scratched him and whipped his two children away from him. Then the country mouse turned to the town mouse, and said: ''Tis thus then that people know you have extended your walls! It is for this that you have acquired your good name! In this fashion is it that you heap favours on your guests! What is my business in your house, accepting and eating the morsels you offer? You are a slave humbler even than my slaves. If you wish it I will free you from your bonds. [At least] my head and appetites are subservient to me. But you are their slaves, you that are even less than I. God has dealt favourably with me, and has entrusted to me the treasure of contentment. Sorrow has been buried away as if it were silver. With each day (God) gives me my daily bread. Like a foolhardy man I forsook my own morsel. But I desire no sweets accompanied by suffering. If you have a taste for contentment, why suffer such trials?'

Whether it is true or not that 'Aṭṭár suffered death at the hands of the Mongols it is impossible to ascertain. The occurrence is at least possible. During his lifetime, roughly contemporary with the Crusades, a people began to assert itself in the east of Asia whose movements were destined to have disastrous effects on the history of the civilized world. Of this people, the Mongols, little had been heard until they were brought into dreadful prominence by the devastation which they wrought under their leader Chingiz (Jenghiz) Khán, the 'Very Mighty King'. This savage general began that career of conquest which sent his name down to history as another 'Scourge of God' only after he had established his lordship over the whole of the nomad confederacy to which his tribe belonged. Then, in the course of twenty years, he overran with his hordes every land from the Yellow Sea to the Danube, leaving a trail of horror in his wake. In Persia the provinces of Khíva, where the enlightened dynasty of Khwárazm Sháhs was established, and Khurásán in all its great extent, were the first to suffer. Their inhabitants were mercilessly slaughtered, their towns plundered and laid in ruins, and their civilization destroyed.

Chingiz died in A.D. 1227, but his tradition and bloodthirsty methods of conquest were carried on by his successors in the Great Khánate. In A.D. 1251 a gathering of Tartar chiefs resolved on two expeditions of further conquests: the first under Ḳubilay Khán (Coleridge's *Kubla Khan*) against China, and the second under Húlágú Khán against Persia, Mesopotamia, Asia Minor, and Syria. Though Syria resisted his efforts, Persia and Mesopotamia were devastated by Húlágú's onslaught as though by a pestilence. On his way westwards he sacked Alamút, the chief stronghold of the Isma'ílí Assassins, and by his destruction of Baghdad in A.D. 1258 he exterminated the 'Abbásid Caliphate, which had for five centuries held at least nominal sway in Persia, and dealt a heavy blow at the Islamic hierarchy.

The Mongol Domination

THE effects of the destruction of the Caliphate were many, the greatest being that Islam was for a time without any generally recognized head, and Persia no longer acknowledged an Arab ruler even nominally, with the important consequence for its literature that Arabic ceased to be the official language and gave way to Persian. Further, Húlágú Khán replaced the various small independent dynasties of Persia by the dynasty of the Íl Khána, of which he was himself the founder, and which united the whole of Persia again under one head. At first the Íl Khán, tribal or provincial Kháns, continued to owe nominal allegiance to the Great Kháns of China. But they did not long maintain even this show of loyalty, and by repudiation of external allegiance the dynasty, which reigned from A.D. 1265-1337, put itself to some extent into sympathy with its subjects. The relationship between prince and people was further improved when the dynasty, under Gházán Khán, renounced paganism and became convert to Islam.

The Íl Kháns gave the country a term of comparative peace, for they made some attempt at ordered government, and were generally strong enough to discourage attack from without. But it is only by comparison with the chaos and horrors that preceded and followed that the state of Persia at the time can be described as ordered or peaceful. The ruling princes were constantly at war with rivals at home, when they were not engaged abroad against rebellious or still unconquered provinces. Few of them died a natural death, and their viziers, generally Persians or Jews, lived in constant terror of torture or assassination. It was a state of affairs which made the ultimate collapse of the Íl Khánate inevitable; and, when it did finally fall, it was succeeded by half a century of complete anarchy, during which time Persia was divided among petty dynasties whose history is obscure and whose territorial possessions were constantly changing their boundaries. The only clear fact that emerges from the confusion—and it is one that fixes the character of the period—is that fratricidal war was the normal concomitant of existence. The chance which this gave to an outside power was seized by a Tartar warrior equal in savage fame with Chingiz Khán—no less a person than Tímúri-Lang (i.e. Tímúr the lame)—Tamerlane—who was then not far away. Tímúr professed to be a Muslim, but there is little to choose between him and the pagan Chingiz for hideous butchery and destructiveness. With Samarḳand as his headquarters he overran Persia and made it the nucleus of a mighty empire, which included Asia Minor, Turkistan, Mesopotamia and all the lands to the Ganges. He was on his way to invade China when he died in A.D. 1405.

Tímúr's reign had been one of terror, but it made for order, though of a kind that could not long survive him. The century which followed was, to quote Professor Browne, 'in its latter part one of those chaotic and anarchical periods which, in Persian history, commonly follow the death of a great conqueror and empire builder'. It is true that the earlier part of the century saw the long and largely peaceful reign of Sháh Rukh (Tímúr's fourth son), and of his son Ulúgh Beg, both of whom can be called sound rulers and patrons of science and letters. But the death of Ulúgh Beg at the hands of his own son marked the beginning of the end of the domination in Persia of Tímúr's line. His descendants carried on a campaign of murder one against the other for possession of the throne; the empire which he had built up was divided piecemeal between the rival claimants within and alien hordes who fell upon it from without, and for the inhabitants of Persia chaos reigned.

In the flood of ruin which the Tartar invasions had poured over Asia and Europe there were yet some seeds of growth and culture. In Europe the Mongols were an indirect cause of the Renaissance, for it was their pressure behind the Ottoman Turks which led to the fall of Constantinople and the consequent spread of Greek learning in Europe. In Persia, though to this day great belts of country have remained ruined and uncultivated, some possibility of spiritual life survived. Islam was never entirely wiped out, for since Chingiz Khán and his immediate successors were heathens, they had no religious views of their own to impose, and mysticism, which flourishes in times of physical adversity, lent fresh strength to Ṣúfíism, at any rate in the south of Persia.

Amongst those who escaped or remained unaffected by the catastrophic events of the time, were two Ṣúfí writers whose works have achieved the utmost popularity in Persia and have also become widely known outside it, namely the mystic Jalálu 'l Dín Rúmí and the moralist Sa'dí of Shíráz. Jalálu 'l Dín was born at Balkh in A.D. 1207. Soon after his birth his father seems to have incurred the jealousy of the ruler of Balkh, who was his kinsman, and was compelled to flee. During the years which followed, the family travelled extensively and settled finally at Ḳoniya (Iconium) in Asia Minor, from the Arabic name of which, 'Rúm', the poet took his pen-name. Legend says that at Níshápúr Jalálu 'l Dín had met the mystical poet Farídu 'l Dín and obtained from him a gift of his *Asrár-náma* (Book of Mysteries). But whether Jalálu 'l Din came under the direct personal influence of the older poet or not, his spiritual indebtedness to him is undoubted, though he was destined to outshine his predecessor in the art of mystical poetry.

Jalálu 'l Dín began his literary career by making himself master of the exact sciences, and seems to have worked undisturbed by the horrors of the Mongol invasion. Finding that the coldness of the sciences did not satisfy his religious needs, he turned to the study of mysticism, under such masters as Burhánu 'l Dín Tirmíẕí, and later under the mysterious wandering dervish known as Shamsi Tabríz. The latter remained with him for several years and exerted over the poet an influence so great that the collection of Jalál's lyrical poems has been known for centuries as the *Díwáni Shamsi Tabríz* (the Díwán of Shamsi Tabríz). The exact reason for this mis-labelling of Jalálu 'l Dín's work is a mystery which has yet to be solved, but it is at any rate an indication of the intimate connexion between the poet and the dervish. When the latter died, suddenly and mysteriously, in A.D. 1247, his pupil was inconsolable, and to perpetuate his memory founded a new order of dervishes. From the founder's Arabic title of 'Mawláná' (Our Master), the order is called that of the *Mawlawí* or, to give the word its better known Turkish pronunciation, the *Mevleví* Dervishes, who are well known to-day as the 'dancing dervishes'. Their 'dance' bears a mystical reference to the movement of the spheres and is technically known as *Samá'*, an Arabic word meaning 'the hearing (of music)', and here also the ecstasy caused thereby.

Inspired by the emotions of the time, Jalálu 'l Dín composed many of his *ghazals*, *rubá'íyát* (quatrains) and *tarjí'-band* (rondeaux) that make up his *díwán*. The poems are full of longing for union with the 'Truth', and dwell without ceasing on the hope of its fulfilment. After Shamsi Tabríz's death and the completion of the *díwán*, the poet began his masterpiece, the *Maṣnawí i Ma'nawí* (Spiritual Maṣnawí), which native commentators have called the 'Ḳur'án in the Pahlawi' (i.e. the Persian) Tongue', a title which accounts for the saying, 'He (Jalálu 'l Dín) is not a prophet, but he has a book'. The *Maṣnawí* is an immense work which contains in its six books all the doctrines, traditions, and legends of Ṣúfíism, presented in a series of parables, allegories, and pseudo-historical narratives. Nearly all of them, including the opening poem, which the late Professor Palmer aptly entitled 'The Song of the Reed', are meant to illustrate the transcendental power of divine love over man and his actions, and to prove that it is for this love that man must seek self-annihilation and union with God. In the author's Arabic introduction to the book he claims, among other things, that it is a 'commentary on the Ḳur'án and a rectifier of morals . . . containing strange and rare anecdotes, the most excellent discourses, and most precious pieces of argument . . . It is the path of ascetics and the garden of the initiated.' Much in the book is obscure and the sequence of thought is not always clear, so that in spite of its set purpose the work must be held to be a piece of poetry often monotonous, rather than a lucid philosophical treatise. In Persia the poem is taken at its face value as a disquisition on Ṣúfíism and is known as '*The* maṣnawí', though *maṣnawí* is but the ordinary term for a poem in rhymed couplets. Here is a prose translation of a characteristic passage from the poem—the story is being told of an ambassador who came from the Emperor of Rúm to visit the Caliph 'Umar—

He was a venerable and perfect man and an eager seeker [after the truth],
He was a man swift of perception taking advantage of a moment,
He saw that leader to salvation ['Umar] that had the power of guiding aright,
That had pure seed in a pure soil.
Said the man to him : 'O Commander of the Faithful,
How does the soul come down to earth from above?
How can so measureless a bird be confined in a cage?'
He replied: 'God speaks fascinating words and stories to the soul,
To things of naught having neither eyes nor ears;
When He speaks His words of fascination they are roused to ferment;
At His words these things of naught very quickly
Are conceived and bound into being.
Again when He speaks His spells to the created things,
He swiftly drives them back into nothingness.
He hints a sign to the body and it becomes soul,
He speaks to the sun and it spreads its rays.
Again, a dreaded hint comes to its ear,
And a hundred eclipses fall upon its face.
He whispers into the ear of the rose and makes it bloom,
He speaks sweetly to the tulip and makes it radiant,
What is it that God called down into the ear of the earth,
Whereon it meditates and remains silent?
What did that Speaker call into the ear of the cloud,
That it pours forth rain-water from its eye like a water-skin?
And if a man is distracted by perplexity,
God has spoken a riddle in his ear
To imprison him between two purposes;
For he says: "Shall I do that or its opposite?"
Also from God comes preference for one alternative;
Of the two he chooses one wing.
If you do not desire the destruction of your soul through perplexity,
Do not press much cotton into the ear of your soul.
Remove the cotton of evil inspiration from your soul
That the cry from heaven may enter your ear,
That you may understand those riddles of His,
That you may perceive His widespread secret.
Thus the ear of the soul becomes the place of inspiration;
And what is inspiration but speech concealed from the senses?
There is no perception of it but to the ear and eye of the soul;
The ear of the mind and the eye of reason are devoid of it.'

The last couplet enunciates one of the main principles of

mysticism, namely that perception of God comes through Divine intuition and not by any process of reasoning. The earlier part of the section is an attempt to solve the problem of man's responsibility for his actions. According to the poet, God is the only real agent, and is responsible for all good and evil in the world, the evil being cancelled out by love. If man is implicitly obedient and keeps his heart open for divine inspiration, he will at all times be acting according to God's will without any contrary impulse.

What follows is the prose translation of an ode from the poet's *Díwán*:

Of myself I was created out of comeliness full of purity, my heart;
I said to thee: Behold how wondrous is the beauty of God, my heart.
Thy slaves are a thousand suns, the eye and the lamp;
Without thy rays souls are in shadow, my heart.
There is an extreme beyond which no beauty passeth,
Yet thy comeliness and grace pass all bounds, my heart.
Fairies and demons gird their loins in service before thee,
Kings bow to thee, and the stars and the heavens, my heart.
What heart is there that beareth not the brand of servitude to thee?
What branded sorrow to which thou art not solace, my heart?
At thy command is every eternal treasure;
What treasure is there which thou holdest not in annihilation?
Withhold not thy regard from them that are consumed with fire, for thy regard
Is as the river of Paradise to heal and quench all burning, my heart.
I said: this moon remains for the Sun of Tabríz [Shamsi Tabríz]
My heart said: Where is he and whither gone, my heart?

The criticism of Jalálu 'l Dín's work pronounced by Dr. R. A. Nicholson is worthy of note. He says in the preface to his *Dīwāni Shamsi Tabrīz*[1]: 'Jalālu 'ddīn lacks the colour and the perfume of Hāfiz, who is by turns grave and gay, blasphemous and devout, serious and ironic; his music is rich and full, but for the most part he plays on one string. . . . As a mystic he was too much in earnest to care for, even if he observed, the incongruities which draw upon him the censure of fastidious critics. As a poet, he sought to invest the Ṣūfī doctrine with every

[1] Cambridge, 1898.

charm that his genius could inspire.' The poet died at Ḳoniya in A.D. 1273.

Sa'dí of Shíráz (*c.* A. D. 1184–1291) was, in his life and works, cast in a very different mould from Jalálu 'l Dín Rúmí's. His philosophy was much more practical and commonplace, and he was a stranger to metaphysics. He excelled in preaching what are ordinarily called the Christian virtues; humility, charity, gentleness, and the like; his exhortations being generally pressed home with anecdotes culled from his own experience. But he was no ascetic and he made no attempt to deny to others the earthly delights which doubtless he himself enjoyed. He was born at Shíráz and was able to spend his student days at the Niẓámiya College at Baghdad, through the generosity of his patron Sa'd ibn Zangí, the Atábeg ruler of Fárs, from whom he derived his pen-name. The Mongol invasion occurred before he could return home, and, after ending his studies, he spent a number of years in travel and adventure in most of the known countries of the world. He visited India, Arabia, and North Africa, and for a time also he lived as a recluse at Jerusalem, until, during a raid by crusaders, he was carried off a prisoner to Tripoli in Syria, where he was set to labour on the fortifications. His ransom was purchased at the expense of a forced marriage with a benefactor's daughter, but the unhappiness of it drove him to seek relief in renewed travel. When he finally returned to his native Shíráz, he found that the south of Persia had been left more or less undisturbed by the Mongols and he was able to find a home at the court of his old patron's son. There he set down at his leisure the results of his varied experiences and enjoyed in comfort the veneration he inspired by his life and writings. The respect in which he was held is marked by his being universally known as 'Shaykh Sa'dí', and often simply as 'The Shaykh'.

Though Sa'dí was a prolific writer in all forms of verse, the works with which his name is universally associated are the *Bústán* (Orchard) and the *Gulistán* (Rose Garden), both of which have introduced themselves by translation into all modern literatures. The *Bústán* contains within its ten sections of facile and often beautiful verse, dissertations on justice, good government, beneficence, earthly and mystic love, humility, submissiveness, contentment, and other excellences. Numerous anecdotes illustrate these virtues in practice by famous personages, saints and warriors, courtiers and kings. His *Gulistán*, written in prose, but with long sections in verse, covers practically the same ground. It is a lighter, more humorous work than the *Bústán*, and like it contains innumerable stories culled from history or from the author's own accumulated experiences. Practical expediency seems to be the ordinary theme of the books, and the ethical character of some of their teaching is not beyond question. Their simplicity, however, has a decided charm, and there is a freshness in their presentation of easily assimilated wisdom that is palatable even to those who have not acquired the stereotyped Oriental taste in this particular. The poet's *díwán* proves that he could write lyrics, elegies, and odes as good of their kind as his didactic verse. Some of his lyrics have even been considered as good as those of Ḥáfiẓ, the greatest of all Persian lyricists; but if that estimate does not apply to all of his poems, their occasional excellence cannot be questioned.

It is more than probable that on his many journeys Sa'dí had assumed the guise of a dervish and had been initiated into one of the orders of wandering dervishes. He has constant anecdotes to retail of their mode of life and their habits, and he frequently employs the jargon of the Ṣúfís. He never ventures, however, to discuss Ṣúfí doctrines with any thoroughness, and for that reason the point of his discourses is more easily and generally comprehensible. The result is that in both East and West his works are exceedingly well known and far more widely popular than those of Jalálu 'l Dín. Sa'dí was an old man when he wrote. The fiery enthusiasms of youth had been tempered by years of varied experience, and it is the product of his ripe wisdom that he presents to his readers. The moral which he appends to the first story in the *Gulistán* illustrates the direction in which that wisdom often lies: 'A lie which mingles good-will is better than a truth which stirs up mischief.' Commonly, however, his praise is given to real virtue, and he delights in picturing ideal instances of ethical conduct. Here is an example from the fourth book of the *Bústán*, 'on Humility':

I remember that Nile, the water-carrier,
One year brought no gift of water to Egypt.
A company of people to the mountains travelled
Praying with loud supplication for rain.
But from their weeping no stream came flowing
Save with the tears from the women's eyes.
News of their plight was brought to Zú 'l Nún,
Saying: 'The people suffer much woe and hardship;
Pray therefore for these unfortunate ones,
For the words of one acceptable to God are not turned aside.'
I heard then that Zú 'l Nún fled to Midian.
No long time passed before rain poured down.
And after twenty days news came to Midian
That the black-hearted cloud had shed tears over them,
Thereupon the saint resolved quickly to return,
For the pools had filled with the spring floods.
In secret an understanding man asked him:
'What wisdom was there in thy going thus?' He replied:
'I heard that upon fowl, ant and beast of prey
Would come sore straits through the deeds of evil men.
In this clime I had observed much,
But saw none more full of sin than I was:
Therefore I went, lest through mine evil
The door of good might be closed against the multitude.'

Sa'dí's dependence on the goodwill of princely patrons accounts for the number of his *ḳaṣídas*, both in Arabic and

Persian, which have survived, and also for a collection of *mutáyabát* (jests), otherwise known as *khabíṣát* (obscene poems). The latter name best indicates the character of the collection, which Sa'dí justified on the ground that princes must be kept amused, and in the fashion which best accords with their desires, though it is only with reluctance that he undertook the task. It speaks well for the poet that his name lives by his more edifying works, upon which he expended greater art and labour.

Sa'dí was fortunate in having a patron who appreciated poetry. The Mongols cared little for any verse that was not concerned with lavish flattery of themselves. On the other hand they recognized the material and practical value of science and history, and consequently the exponents of these subjects received ample encouragement. Amongst those who had made a name before the coming of the Mongols was the philosopher, astronomer, and mathematician Naṣíru 'l Dín of Ṭús († 1274). He was in the service of the last Grand Master of the Assassins when Húlágú sacked their capital Alamút. Knowing that the astronomer could be of use to him, the Mongol conqueror spared his life and made him his adviser. In that capacity he accompanied Húlágú on his expedition against Baghdad, and when the Mongol capital was temporarily set up at Marágha in Aẕarbayján, Naṣír, who had by that time acquired great influence with his master, was there able to erect an observatory, which he made famous. The majority of his works on philosophy, astronomy, theology, &c., were written in Arabic, for he was a product of the 'Abbásid rather than of the Mongol period. But he also wrote in his native Persian and composed in that tongue his best-known book, the *Akhláḳi Náṣirí* (Náṣirí Ethics), on practical philosophy, and further the *Zíjí Ílkháni* (The Ílkhán Astronomical Tables)—composed at Marágha for Húlágú

Khán—and various other treatises on philosophy, astronomy, and so forth. He appears also to have written some poetry, of which not much has survived, and a book on prosody, *Mi'yáru 'l Ash'ár* (Touchstone of Poetry), has been ascribed to him. The verdict of history on Naṣíru 'l Dín is a most unfavourable one. It might have been expected that the conduct of a man of his undoubted mental qualities would have been regulated by some standard higher than that of personal advantage. Yet he appears not only to have betrayed his Isma'ílí master to Húlágú, but to have been instrumental in bringing the last Caliph treacherously to his death at the hands of the Mongols. His chief contribution to letters, the *Akhláḳi Náṣirí*, is perhaps the best work on ethics in the whole of Islamic literature, but it is significant of its author's character that the book is provided with two prefaces. The first of these belauds the Isma'ílís, for the book was written for Náṣiru 'l Dín Muhtasham, the Isma'ílí governor of Kúhistán, after whom the book is named; the second and later preface thanks a beneficent prince for having delivered him from the hands of these 'Heretics' (*muláḥida*). Some of the chapter headings provide a general idea of the contents of *Akhláḳi Náṣirí*, the difficult style of which is trying and confusing to the reader. The first of the three main portions, into which the work is divided, is headed 'On moral refinement', and contains such sections as 'On knowledge of the human soul', 'On perfection and deficiency of the human soul', and 'On the good and on happiness, which are the aims of perfection'. The second main division contains chapters 'On the knowledge of policy and the administration of revenues', 'On good manners in speech', 'On good manners in eating', and so forth. The last part concerns itself with the art of government and on the laws which regulate the intercourse between man and man. There is as yet no

European edition or translation of the work, though the much later and inferior *Akhláḳi Jalálí* has found translators into English.

Amongst the disciples of Naṣír was Ḳutbu 'l Dín (†A.D. 1310), who belonged to a family of physicians of Shíráz. He had spent most of his time at Mongol courts, and, like his master, produced in Arabic a number of works on philosophy, medicine, and astronomy; but is best known for an encyclopaedia of the sciences. Along with Naṣíru 'l Dín, Húlágú Khán had taken with him on his expeditions the historian 'Aṭá Malik (†1283) of Juwayn, a village in Níshápúr. As Húlágú's secretary he marched with him against the Isma'ílís and afterwards against Baghdad, of which he became governor. In his *Ta'ríkh i Jahán-gushá* (History of the World Conqueror) (i.e. Chingiz Khán), after dealing with earlier Mongol history, he recounts the various events which took place during the reigns and campaigns of Chingiz Khán and Húlágú Khán down to the expedition against the Isma'ílís, of whom the book contains a full and circumstantial account of great interest. To 'Aṭá Malik, the Persian geographer and cosmographer Ḳazwíní dedicated his Arabic treatise *'Ajá'ibu 'l Makhlúḳát* (The Wonders of Creation), a subject with which he also dealt in another work of the same type, the *'Áṣáru 'l Bilád* (Monuments of the Countries). Neither work is very scientific, even as judged by the standards of the author's own day, but they contain much that is of topographical and biographical interest. 'Aṭá Malik himself was a man of considerable importance at the Mongol court. He possessed great political acumen, and though nominally only the deputy of the governor of Iráḳ, in reality he held the reins of the government of Baghdad and the surrounding districts in his own hands. His success aroused jealousy in not a few quarters, one case having an interesting consequence. Amongst the detractors of the politician-historian was the father of Ibnu 'l Ṭiḳṭaḳí, author of the *Kitábu 'l Fakhrí*, that excellently written manual of Arabic history and politics. The elder Ibnu 'l Ṭiḳṭaḳí endeavoured to obtain the dismissal of the governor, who revenged himself by having him assassinated. The murdered man's son gives full vent in the *Fakhrí* to his outraged feelings, and it is not surprising that 'Aṭá Malik is scarcely mentioned in the book without some disparaging remark.

From 'Aṭá Malik's day until the accession of Gházán Khán, Húlágú's great-grandson, in A.D. 1295, there was but small literary activity. The reign of Gházán, though short, was marked by internal security and success in war against external foes, a position of affairs which was brought about largely by the efforts of the great statesman and historian Rashídu 'l Dín Faẓlu 'lláh, who was his vizier. Rashíd had begun his career as physician to Abáḳá Khán, Húlágú's son, and was ultimately induced by Gházán Khán to become his vizier. His activities were extensive. In spite of his many duties of state he found time to compile the *Jámi'u 'l Tawáríkh* (Compendium of Histories), one of the best and most elaborate of those histories of the world with which Persian literature abounds. The work seems to have been inspired by Gházán Khán, whose object was to leave to posterity a monument of the Mongol exploits, and was continued by Rashídu 'l Dín in the reign of Gházán's brother and successor, Uljaytú Khán, to whom Rashíd also acted as vizier. The work is divided into two parts. The first is a special history of the Turks and Mongols from the earliest times to the end of the reign of Gházán Khán ; the second part, besides a section on the history of Uljaytú's reign, contains a general history of the world from the Creation down to the first years of the reign of Uljaytú. Included in it are accounts of the Caliphate, of the dynasties of the Ghaznawids, Saljúḳs, and Khwárizm-sháhs, and of the Isma'ílís. Other nations of the world are represented by the legendary rulers of the ancient Turks, by the Chinese, the Israelites, the Franks, and Indians. The author seems to have derived much of his material by hearsay from many sources. For instance, when dealing with the Franks, he sets down a somewhat curious and not generally accepted version of Christianity, which he probably obtained from the followers of some heresy, and in the history of the Jews a Midrashic account of the Creation is given instead of the ordinary narrative of the Book of Genesis.

Indeed he expounds his methods in his introduction to the history of the Israelites, where he says: 'The essential condition for a historian is that he should write the history of each people according to their own claims and should express no opinion of his own concerning them, either in exaggeration or palliation. Whether they be true or false he must set them down exactly in accordance with the intention and claim of each people, so that responsibility for exaggeration or palliation, for truth or falsehood, may rest upon their intentions and not upon the historian. This theory is repeated here so that if anything be found incomprehensible or unaccountable, the humble historian be not taken to task therefor, nor have the tongue of blame lengthened against him, but rather his intention shall be held blameless by reason of these principles; if it please God Almighty.'

His account of the creation is as follows:

The first things which God Almighty created were the heavens and the earths and what exists between the two, such as the heavenly hosts and the armies of the earths—thus, speaking generally. The details are, that on Sunday light and darkness and the four elements [earth, air, fire, water] came into existence; light became particular to the heavens and darkness to the finite world. On that day also time was divided into night and day, and the holy angels and spiritual beings were created.

On Monday the elements were composed, temperament was revealed, and hell was created.

On Tuesday vegetable growths in all their various states were created, namely ground herbage, grass, and trees. Also heaven was created on that day, after God had at dawn gathered all the waters into one place and called them 'sea'. Also he drove some of the waters into river courses, so that the surface of the earth appeared and parts of it were dried and became capable of cultivation.

On Wednesday he created the sun, moon, and other heavenly bodies, and endowed them with light. And he made the sun the agent of day and the conqueror of darkness, and the moon the agent of night. To each of them he gave special qualities of different kinds in the physical world.

On Thursday he created two families in the animal world—birds and fishes; that is, the animals of the air and of the water such as fowl, fish, and so forth.

On Friday, at the first hour he created all animals that exist on the surface of land, at the second hour he created Adam, upon whom be peace, the human being perfect in form and in essence, distinguished from the rest in his creation and his quality, wise, understanding, righteous, reasonable, having the power of deep thought and of administration and able to conceive the true values of beings by means of divine inspiration. At that hour too a great bird descended from heaven and settled on the shore of the sea and cried out: 'O ye birds and fishes, be warned, for God hath now with his own might created upon this earth an animal strange and wonderful, having majesty and grandeur. He hath set upon him the name "man" and hath planted in him overwhelming power whereby he may bring down fowl from the air or bring up fish from the depth of the sea, by command of God, Most High. Also he hath put his blessing upon his children, offspring, and kindred, and in the whole race of them whose name is "man" he hath established the power to propagate and generate, by his own command, may he be aggrandized and exalted, that their children may be many and without number and their existence may be the cause of the endurance and continuation of the world's prosperity.'

The historian then relates how Adam was admitted into Eden and permitted to eat of all in the garden save the fruit of the tree of knowledge, which he was not even to approach, 'for it finds destruction and nothingness in the Torah', and how Eve was created. The narrative continues with the story of the temptation of Eve by the serpent and of Adam's eating the apple. 'And at the eighth hour of Friday, God ejected Adam from the paradise on the same day that he had created him.' The work is only brought down to the year A.D. 1305, though Rashídu 'l Dín lived until A.D. 1318. In that year Abú Sa'íd, Uljaytú's son and successor, accused the minister of having slain his sovereign, dismissed him from office, and put him to death after confiscating his property.

Court historians under Mongol rulers appear to have filled the place that court poets occupied under the Ghaznawids and Saljúḳs. In A.D. 1317 there was dedicated to Sultán Abú Sa'íd a history entitled *Ta'ríkhi Banákití* (Banákití's history), which was to all intents a summary of Rashídu 'l Dín's 'Compendium of Histories' brought down to the date of Abú Sa'íd's accession. The author, Fakhrí Banákití, was something of a poet as well as a historian, though too little of his verse has survived to enable criticism to be made.

Shortly after the completion of the *Jámi'u 'l Tawáríkh* (The Compendium of Histories), the further record of the history of the Mongols which had been begun by 'Aṭá Maliki Juwayní in the *Ta'ríkh i Jahán-gushá* was resumed in the *Ta'ríkh i Waṣṣáf* (The Panegyrist's History), otherwise known as *Tajziyatu 'l Amṣár* (The Distribution of Cities). This was the work of one of Rashídu 'l Dín's clients known as 'Waṣṣáf' (the Panegyrist), and its chief claim to notice is that it was written with the express purpose of rhetorical display. The book, is as a consequence, an absurdly bombastic composition, in which sense is concealed in multitudes of words, and history is subordinated to verbal conceit. The number of writers, particularly in India, who adopted this euphuistic method of composition, was so great that it had its effect in Europe, where to this day the common idea of Persian prose is that its characteristics are ordinarily those of the most florid 'Babu' English. It may be of interest to compare the style with that of some less artificially written work. Here, for example, is a fairly close translation of the beginning of the passage in the

Ta'ríkh i Waṣṣáf which describes the Mongol capture of Baghdad:

They that examine the records of the incidents of all ages and they that are acquainted with the contents of the pages of events, the unveilers of the countenance of the virgins of novelty, and they that show forth the changes of the months and centuries (may Alláh encompass them all with his wide mercy!) have testified thus: The City of Peace [Baghdad] in the time of the 'Abbásid Caliphs was ever guarded from the hardships and ills of fortune in the sanctuary of safety and security. It was the envy of all the emperors of the world, and its palaces and mansions shared secrets with the æther of the skies. Its surrounding districts and adjacent lands were equal with the Garden of Blessings in pleasantness and freshness. In its air and in its open spaces the bird of security and peace was for ever flying, and in it were blessings and delights of every kind, comforts and luxuries of every variety, so that the mind in wonderment is incapable of enumerating them.

Khiẕr's draught is Baghdad's water,
Moses' fire is there at Baghdad,
Egypt's capital naught becomes,
When Baghdad's prime encounters it.

Its schools and colleges are filled with champions of the rarest learning. In those days discord went with tied hands and broken feet. The masters of the various crafts and arts, in the greatness of their skill, were such that they could limn sparks of fire upon running water, and in its zeal for true portraiture the pen of slander broke from shame when it touched paper.

Compare this with the simplicity and directness of Rashídu 'l Dín when engaged in describing the Mongol descent on Baghdad:

On the ninth of Ẕú 'l Ḥijja in the year 655 . . . having crossed the Tigris they came to the edge of the 'Ísá canal. Súnjak Núyán begged Manjú for the command of the advanced troops that were to operate to the west of Baghdad, and when permission was given he marched away and reached Ḥurmat. Mujáhidu 'l Dín Dawátdár, who was in command of the Caliph's army, and Ibn Karz had encamped between Ya'ḳúbiya and Bájisra. When they heard that the Mongols had reached the west bank they crossed the Tigris . . . and joined battle with the Mongol army. . . . In that district [of Dujayl] there was a great sheet of water. The Mongols cut the dykes surrounding it so that the whole of the near forces of the Baghdad army were overwhelmed by the water. Buḳá Tímúr at sunrise on Thursday, the 10th of Muḥarram, attacked Dawátdár and Ibn Karz and victoriously put the Baghdad army to flight.

Another work of note, not quite so artificially elaborated as the foregoing, owed its inspiration to Rashídu 'l Dín, namely, the *Ta'ríkh i Guzída* (Select History) of Ḥamdulláh Mustawfí, who dedicated it to Rashídu 'l Dín's son, Ghiyáṣu 'l Dín. In it the author seeks to trace the origins and general history of the Persian dynasties, of Islam, and of the notable protagonists of Muḥammadanism, covering the whole period from the beginning of creation down to the date of the completion of the book in A.D. 1330. Ḥamdulláh is further responsible for a rhymed chronicle of events from the time of Muḥammad, entitled *Ẓafar-náma* (Book of Victory), which is a direct imitation and continuation of the *Sháh-náma*. In addition to the two historical works mentioned, Ḥamdulláh compiled a cosmographical and geographical work called *Nuzhatu 'l Ḳulúb* (Hearts' Delight). This contains various sections which deal, according to the ideas of the time, with the origin and composition of the universe, and also, in one section, treats more particularly of the geography of Persia and of some neighbouring countries. Almost at the same time as Ḥamdulláh's *Ẓafar-náma* appeared Aḥmad Tabrízí's *Sháhansháh-náma*, which is a versified history of Chingiz Khán and his successors down to A.D. 1338. Artistically the work is by no means the equal of the *Ẓafar-náma*, which is a contrast, both in its subject-matter and the excellence of its style, to most of the innumerable imitations of the *Sháh-náma*. The *Sháhansháh-náma* is a fairly good specimen of such imitations; the majority are hyperbolical enconiums written for rich patrons who were obviously expected to reward the compositions with substantial gifts.

In the realm of poetry little was being produced during the Ílkháni period. In India, it is true that the inspiration of Niẓámí of Ganja was still alive. Amír Khusraw of Delhi, who died in A.D. 1325, composed a *Khamsa* (quintet) of romantic poems almost as fine as Niẓámí's own, and he was in addition an epic and lyric poet of no mean order.

But he belongs to Indian rather than to Persian literature, for he was born and lived in India, and his genius cannot be put to the credit of Mongol Persia.

The most successful imitator that Niẕámí had in his own country seems to have been Khwájú of Kirmán (1281–1352). This poet in the course of his career, favoured with his services a number of patrons belonging to the various dynasties which sprang up after the fall of the Íl Kháns. His 'Quintet' of romantic poems follows fairly closely the copy set by Niẕámí, and is in fact the first imitation by a Persian of which there is any trace. It includes, in addition to the poems on the stereotyped love themes of legend such as the story of 'Humay and Humayún' and that of 'Gul and Nawrúz', an ethical poem entitled *Rawẕatu 'l Anwár* (Garden of Fires), which had for its model Niẕámí's *Makhzanu 'l Asrár* (Treasure-house of Secrets). The Quintet was not Kirmání's only work, for he began his career as a panegyrist and composed many *ḳaṣídas* in praise of his patrons at the court of the Muẕaffarís and at the rival court of Abú Isḥáḳ at Shíráz. Various odes, quatrains, &c., which are included in his *díwán*, are also to be placed to his credit.

Ṣúfí literature is well represented in the later years of the Íl Khán dynasty and during the disturbed interval of half a century which preceded Tímúri Lang's (Tamerlane's) conquest of Persia. Two widely-known works of the period, both dealing with mystical subjects, are the *Lama'át* (Flashes) of 'Iráḳí (who died about A.D. 1288) and the *Gulshani Ráz* (Rose Garden of Mystery), composed by Maḥmúd of Shabistar († A.D. 1320). The *Lama'át* is a treatise in mixed prose and verse dealing with the various stages of mystical love. It was inspired by the Arab mystic Ibnu 'l 'Arabí and was brought into special notice, about a century and a half after its composition, by the famous poet Jámí who wrote a commentary on it. Its subject-matter does not differ in essence from that of the 'Spiritual Maṣnawi' of Jalálu 'l Dín Rúmí, but the treatment of the different stages of mystical love is new. During a life of travel and study 'Iráḳí visited Asia Minor, India, Egypt, and Syria, and composed, in addition to the *Lama'át*, a *díwán* containing many fine *ghazals* and other poems. Many of the *ghazals* are of that erotic character which is almost inevitable when songs of mystical love must be sung in terms representing physical attraction. Even Ḥáfiẓ dealing with divine love has not escaped the charge of eroticism, though he has not gone to the same lengths as 'Iráḳí in his methods of representation.

The *Gulshani Ráz* has enjoyed amongst Ṣúfís a great reputation as a manual of their creed. It is a poem in the *maṣnawí* form, composed in answer to a number of questions on Ṣúfiism, which are included in the text of the poem. The answers, which are illustrated by many anecdotes and parables, elucidate the essential doctrines of that system of mysticism and attempt to illumine its more recondite aspects. The mystical poem entitled *Jám i Jam* (The Cup of Jamshíd), also deserves mention in this connexion. It was written during the period of the interregnum by Awḥadí († A.D. 1337) of Marágha (where Húlágú for a time had his capital) in imitation of the *Ḥadíḳatu 'l Ḥaḳíḳa* of the poet Saná'í, and became very popular.

Two rival dynasties that arose after the fall of the Íl Kháns take the credit of having given their patronage to the three most notable writers of their day—one of them the greatest poet in Persian literature. These two dynasties were the Ílkáns or Jalá'irs of 'Iráḳ and the Muẓaffarís of Shíráz. The founder of the Jalá'irs, Shaykh Ḥasani Buzurg (the Great) and his son and successor Shaykh Uways, were able, even during the political chaos of the time, to devote some attention to letters. At his court at Baghdad Shaykh Uways gave a position to 'Ubaydi Zákání († 1370–1), a worthy successor in the art of coarse satirical verse to the satirist Súzani, who had lived in Sultan Sanjar's day. Rabelaisian features are encountered fairly frequently, and not unnaturally, in Persian literature, but 'Ubayd seems to have found in coarse lasciviousness a special means of adding effect to his satires both in prose and verse. Of his prose works his *Akhláḳu 'l Ashráf* (Morals of the Nobility), parodied such textbooks of conventional ethics as the *Akhláḳi Náṣirí*; his *Ta'rifát* (Definitions), were a series of epigrams mocking at the everyday life and religion of his time; while his *Risála 'i Rísh* (Epistle on the Beard), is a further piece of sarcastic criticism on similar topics. In his *Hazaliyát* (Ribald Poems) he collected a number of compositions which he wrote in prose and verse, both in Arabic and Persian, and which are for the most part exercises in coarse and obscene humour. Apart from this collection his powers of originality are seen to best advantage in a short humorous poem written in mock-epic style, and entitled *Músh u Gurba* (The Mouse and the Cat). This is a short sketch which uses cats and mice Aesop-fashion, but with a trenchant humour worthy of a Dean Swift. His vein of satire is illustrated by the following story taken from a short collection in a Bodleian manuscript:

The Caliph Mahdí was once separated from his retinue in the hunting-field, and when night fell came to an Arab's hut. The Arab brought him what he had at hand, namely, a jug of wine. When the prince had taken the first drink, he said: 'I am one of Mahdí's attendants.' Taking a second drink, he said: 'I am of Mahdí's generals.' At the third drink, he said: 'I am Mahdí.' On hearing this, the Arab took the jug away from him, saying: 'First you drank and said you were in Mahdí's service. When you drank the second time you claimed to be a general, and now at the third drink you call yourself the Caliph. If you drink again you'll claim to be God.'

'Ubayd's brilliance in the realm of satire was equalled by his contemporary Salmán of Sáwa († 1376 or 1377) in that of panegyric. He was court poet both to Shaykh Ḥasani Buzurg and to Shaykh Uways. For the latter he wrote a *Firáḳ-náma* (Book of Separation), to console him for the loss of a favourite courtier, and also dedicated to him a romantic *maṣnawí, Jamshíd u Khwurshíd.* The latter poem had the merit of introducing new characters into the conventional themes of romantic love which had been steadily following for over a century and a half the stock pattern set by Niẓámí, but Salmán did not venture to give fresh turns to the erotic adventures of his main characters. He also wrote some polished odes, and he excelled in the composition of cunningly contrived *ḳaṣídas.* One well-known example of these highly artificial poems is so written that the initial letters of the verses form an acrostic, while variously marked words in the body of the verses make up other verses having different metres and having the words arranged in some mechanical order of their letters. By contrast with this display of verbal tricks some of his poems are marked by a grace and lucidity which few of his predecessors had displayed. In some of his work he constantly foreshadowed the tropes turned to such excellent account by the mighty Ḥáfiẓ, who was more or less his contemporary.

Here is one of his odes:

Thou that puttest the motes of life in the air of loveliness;
Thou that makest Eden's garden fragrant with thy comeliness;
With the weeping of thy lovers now is Heaven's blue sky torn.
Thou art pale, for through the sunshine's crimson blood thy robe is drawn.
Were the earth of all life's fabric metamorphosed into wind,
Whole I'd see it if but one speck on thy vesture I could find.
From the wine of thy red lips comes a frenzy to all heads,
At the teasing of thy bright eyes, fierce war on all sides spreads.
If in Heav'n and here the loved one in her beauty have no peer
Then only he that is peerless as a lover may draw near.
'Tis not given to any fox on the road of love to start;
On love's path none but heroes walk, Titans with lion-like heart.

This heart holds nought but pain of thee, thou fill'st my head with
 ferment.
Tumult reigns in every head and all men's hearts hold torment.
Cold is my sigh with grief, my heart boils with the blood of anguish.
Thus Salmán in the extremes of both heat and cold doth languish.

Ḥáfiẓ, or to give him his full name, Muḥammad Shamsu 'l Dín Ḥáfiẓ, was the protégé during part of his life of Sháh Shuja', a member of the Muẓaffarí dynasty, who were the rivals of the Jalá'irs. The known details of the poet's life are few. His *nom de guerre* 'Ḥáfiẓ' (one that has the Ḳur'án by heart), implies that he had devoted much time to the study of the Ḳur'án—a fact borne out by indications in his poems. It seems certain too that he spent most of his life in his native town of Shíráz and that he died there—according to the chronogram on his tombstone—in the year 794 of the Hijra, which corresponds to A.D. 1389 or 1390. Two years before Ḥáfiẓ died, Shíráz had fallen to the redoubtable Tímúri Lang and the biographers relate that the Tartar chief then made the acquaintance of the poet. Their statements are difficult to substantiate, for the poet himself does not mention the incident.

It is difficult at this time of day to say anything that is new of the poetry of Ḥáfiẓ. In depth of vision, felicity of language, and beauty of imagery he stands easily and incomparably first amongst the poets of Persia. He wrote *ḳaṣídas* and *rubá'iyát* (quatrains) as well as odes, but it is in the latter that he excelled. His genius lies not so much in the production of original ideas—for he sings of the old themes of love, wine and the beauty of Nature—but the ideas are moulded afresh and his poems display 'a new form and colouring . . . given to the actions of the real world by the artist's imagination'. His sweetest songs are, like those of other poets, not those of the attainment of love's desire but rather of the sorrows of disappointed love, the object of such affection being visualized as a young and beautiful youth on the verge of manhood. Except for an occasional eulogy of some patron there is little of topical or contemporary interest in Ḥáfiẓ's poetry, and all the turmoil of the days in which he lived seldom forced him out of his detachment to make comment thereon in his verses. Ḥáfiẓ is the last of the great Ṣúfí poets. To his fellow-Ṣúfís, who see some mystical reference even in his most sensuous verses, he is known by the Arabic title of *Lisánu 'l Ghayb* (The Tongue of the Hidden). It may be true that a mystical interpretation is required by many of the odes, but some are marked by a realism which makes it impossible not to suspect that the poet sings of some charmer of flesh and blood or of a flask of good wine, rather than of the ethical intoxication of Divine love. A possible reason for the diversity of explanations is that Ḥáfiẓ, like 'Umar Khayyám, used the metaphors and figures of Ṣúfíism to add colour to his work. His poems were collected after his death by his friend Muḥammad Gulandám and achieved a vast popularity which has been accepted without criticism till the present day. Amongst them are a couple of short *maṣnawís* entitled *Sáḳí-náma* and various *kit'as* (fragments). From the number of translations made of his poems Ḥáfiẓ is very familiar, but it may not be out of place to quote an ode, so that his work may not go unrepresented here:

Thus spoke at dawn the field-bird to the newly wakened rose:
'Be kind, for many a bloom like you in this meadow grows'.
The rose laughed: 'You will find that we at truth show no distress,
But never did a lover with harsh words his love so press.
If ruby wine from jewelled cup it is your wish to drink,
Then pearls and corals pierced with eyelash you must strive to link.
Love's savour to his nostrils to entice he ne'er can seek,
Who on the tavern's earthy floor has not swept dusty cheek.'

In Iram's garden yesternight, when, in the grateful air,
The breeze of coming day stirred the tress of hyacinth fair,
I asked: 'Throne of Jamshíd, where is thy world-revealing cup?'
It sighed: 'That waking fortune deep in sleep lies muffled up.'

They are not always words of love that from the tongue descend:
Come, bring me wine, O taverner, and to this talk put end.
His wit and patience to the waves are cast by Ḥáfiẓ' tears.
What can he do, that may not hide how love his being sears?

Here also is Ḥáfiẓ' Will.

If toping be true cause of my demise,
Then bring me to my grave in toper's guise.
In vine-wood casket make my last abode,
And put my grave beside the tavern road.
My corse with tavern-water let them lave;
On toper's shoulder bear me to the grave.
With ruby wine let them my dust allay,
And for sole mourning rite the rebeck play.
And, when I die—this is my testament—
Let only mime or minstrel make lament.
But thou, Ḥáfiẓ, from wine turn not away;
Sultáns no impost on the drunken lay.

The end of the interregnum and its half-dozen antagonistic dynasties was brought about by the invasion of the barbarous Tímúri Lang soon after the beginning of A.D. 1381. In the course of his campaigns the invader destroyed what little had been built up since the former Mongol wave swept over the country, and he further laid in ruins towns and districts which had escaped the first cataclysm. This time, the south of Persia, including Isfahán and Shíráz, was overrun and Baghdad once more occupied.

As under the Íl Kháns so in the Tímúrid period the writing of history constituted the main effort of literary men. No historian of the first order, however, can be claimed for that age, though a number of inferior compilers have left works behind them. Ḥáfiẓi Abrú is perhaps the best known. He was a member of the courts of Tímúr and of his son Sháh-rukh, and wrote an enormous work on universal history entitled *Zubdatu 'l Tawáríkh* (Cream of Histories), and another on the geography of Persia, neither of which has been wholly preserved. Other historians of Tímúr and of his successors were Niẓámi Shámí and

Sharafu 'l Dín 'Alí Yazdí, each of whom wrote a *Ẓafar-náma* (Book of Victory). Sharafu 'l Dín copied his work almost entirely from Shámí and, though in many ways he improved upon his predecessor, his style contains all the worst faults associated with Persian prose of the florid type. Of far greater importance were Abdu 'l Razzáḳ († 1482) of Samarḳand, and Mírkhwánd († 1498) of Harát. Abdu 'l Razzáḳ's work *Matla'u 'l Sa'dayn* (The Rise of the Two Auspicious Planets), the name of which is more familiar than that of its author, is based on the *Zubdatu 'l Tawáríkh* of Ḥáfiẓi Abrú. Beginning with the reign of Sultán Abú Sa'íd, the Íl Khán monarch and great-grandson of Húlágú, it gives the history of Tímúr and his descendants down to the year A.D. 1470. The later historian Mírkh-wánd was the author of a universal history known as *Rawẓatu 'l Ṣafá* (Garden of Purity). In spite of its pompous and overloaded style and the occasional unreliability of its statements it is the most quoted work of its kind in Persian. Its full title, *Rawẓatu 'l Ṣafá fí Sírati 'l Anbiyá wa 'l Mulúk wa 'l Khulafá*, or the 'Garden of Purity, concerning the History of the Prophets, Kings, and Caliphs', indicates the contents of the work, which is a compilation of vast extent, put together at the instance of the famous vizier, Mír 'Alí Shír Nawá'í, to whom it is dedicated. The history commences with the Creation and deals with Muḥammad, the Imáms and Caliphs; then with the minor dynasties of Persia contemporary with and successors of the 'Abbásids; and finally with the reigns of Chingiz and Tímúr with their respective successors down to Sultán Abú Sa'íd who died in A.D. 1460. The work is concluded by a special history of Sultán Ḥusayn the last of the Tímúrids of Persia, who had Mír 'Alí Shír as his vizier. A geographical appendix completes the whole.

The Tímúrid period was not without its poets and

mystics. Their work, with the brilliant exception of that of Jámí, is generally neither of the first rank nor of any originality, for the reason possibly that it received little encouragement. In lyrical poetry the lead set by Ḥáfiẓ was followed by several poets, of whom Kamál of Khujand († A.D. 1400) and Mullá Muḥammad Shírín Maghribí of Tabríz († A.D. 1406/7) stand out from the rest, though the latter by his mysticism more nearly approaches the spirit of the great lyricist of Shíráz. Kátibí of Níshápúr, who spent some time as a panegyrist at Harát in the reigns of Tímúr and his successor Sháh-rukh, was far more productive and of wider capabilities than these. His *ḳaṣídas*, however, did not draw at Harát the appreciation which he demanded, and he is later found at the courts of Shírwán and Astarabád. There, in addition to *ḳaṣídas*, he turned to the composition of *maṣnawís* of mystical content, and he left three works of this form which appear to be part of an uncompleted *khamsa* after the pattern of Niẓámí's. He died between A.D. 1434 and 1436.

A fellow poet with him at Harát was Mu'ínu 'l Dín Ḳásimi Anwár, whose death-date is probably A.D. 1434. Ḳásim in addition to being an able poet won a reputation as a Shí'a saint and made no less than four pilgrimages on foot to the holy places in Arabia. He appears also to have been a Ṣúfí for he wrote a *maṣnawí*, *Anísu 'l 'Árifín* (The Gnostics' Familiar), which expounds a number of conventional Ṣúfí terms. His saintliness did not protect him from a charge of having being concerned in an attempted assassination of his patron Sháh-rukh, for which he was compelled to leave Harát for Khurásán; though another account says that he left in order to escape the vituperation of his colleagues. His *díwán* contains poems in most of the usual verse-forms, and, in addition, he wrote a number of prose essays, mainly of theological content. Some of his poetry displays the same piety as these prose pieces, as is shown in the following prose translation of an ode taken from his *díwán* (Bodley MS. Elliott 71):

This delight of love is the mark of God's grace,
And all of it is favour beyond our deserts.
The hurt which from thee weighed upon our sore hearts,
Is in form an evil, but in essence a gift.
From all eternity I have been bewildered and intoxicated with love;
This too comes from Heaven's past grace.
In the ecstasy of 'I am the Truth' that came from Him, there went to the stake[1]—
Manṣúr, who was chief in the circle of the God-intoxicated.
Each man runs and goes a step or two [in his life]
Whether he be God-intoxicated or a man of lust.
At every incident which he beholds on his perilous path,
[He cries] 'Beware', 'Come not nigh', 'How is it?', and 'Why comes it?'
The heart of Ḳásim rejoices ever in thy bounties.
Thy majesty lies ever in bounty, truth and purity.

Of a very different type are two satirical versifiers and parodists of the school of 'Ubayd i Zákání. These are Abú Isḥáḳ (or Búsháḳ), the poet of food, and his imitator, Maḥmúd Ḳárí, the poet of clothes. Abú Isḥáḳ, the prototype of the French gastronomist Brillat-Savarin, devoted himself to the composition of odes and quatrains which, in a parody of the lyric style, sing the delights of various culinary products and processes. His collection of these poems goes by the title of *Kanzu 'l Ishtihá* (Treasure of Appetite), and has a preface in which the author explains his reasons for undertaking the composition of them. One may quote from the excellent summary of this given in Rieu's *Catalogue of Persian Manuscripts in the British Museum*: 'He was ambitious to achieve renown in poetry, but coming after so many great poets, as the last of whom he mentions Kamál Khujandí and Ḥáfiẓ, he was at a loss to know what new theme to select, when his beloved came

[1] The actual meaning of the separate words is somewhat obscure, but the general meaning in this line and the next is clearly a reference to Manṣúri Ḥalláj, the early Ṣúfí who suffered death for exclaiming 'I am the Truth' (i.e. God). See p. 35.

in and suggested one by complaining of the loss of her appetite, for the restoration of which he wrote the present work.'

The *Díwán i Albisa* (Sartorial Díwán) of Ḳárí belongs to a period a century and a half later than the work of Abu Isḥáḳ, but its style and subject matter are in direct imitation of the earlier work, and on that account justify its mention here.

The often-quoted biographical work of Dawlatsháh, known as *Taẕkiratu 'l Shu'ará* (Memoir of the Poets), belongs to the days of the last Tímúrid prince. It contains much matter that is original and of value for the lives and works of the earlier poets, but its author is notoriously inaccurate in historical details, so that his work is not always to be trusted. The 'Memoir' was dedicated to that generous patron of letters and scholarship, Mír 'Alí Shír Nawá'í, who gathered round him the most brilliant littérateurs of the day, and to whom is due the inspiration of their finest efforts. The spirit abroad at the court of Sultan Ḥusayn, whose minister Mír 'Alí Shír was, is indicated by the fact that the prince himself wrote a series of ornate panegyrics under the guise of biographies, in a volume called *Majálisu 'l 'Ushsháḳ* (Séances on the (Mystic) Lovers). Mír 'Alí Shír was himself a poet and the biographer of poets. He wrote mainly in the Chaghatay dialect of Turkish, but also composed verse in Persian, and hence fills a definite place in Persian literature. His biographical prose work written in Turki, *Majális u'l Nafá'is*, or 'Séances on Delightful Subjects', deals with the lives of poets contemporary with the author. It was translated into Persian, under the title of *Laṭá'if-náma*, some years after the author's death. A noteworthy client of this Maecenas was Husayn Wá'izi Káshifí, the author of *Anwári Suhayli* (the Lights of Canopus), that widely known, but bombastic and diffuse, Persian translation of *Kalíla wa Dimna*. His original work is represented by a treatise, *Akhláḳ i Muḥsiní*, written after the style of a similar, earlier, and much better known work entitled *Akhláḳ i Jaláli*, the author of which was Muḥammad ibn Asad Dawáni (†1506), who in his turn had imitated the *Akhláḳ i Náṣirí* of Naṣíru 'l Dín Ṭúsí.

The greatest of Mír 'Alí Shír's clients and the most versatile writer of the Tímúrid period, namely, Mullá Núru 'l Dín Abdu 'l Raḥmán Jámí, was born in the village of Jám in Khurásán in A.D. 1414, and from it took the pen-name of 'Jámí', one of the most notable in Persian literature. It has been said that the Persians consider their seven greatest poets to be Firdawsí for epic poetry, Niẓámí for romances, Rúmí for mystical poetry, Sa'dí for his verses on ethical subjects, Ḥáfiẓ for lyrics, and Jámí for general excellence in all these forms. Though such generalization must be treated with caution, it is a near approximation to the truth. As for Jámí himself, though he is not, as is often said, 'the last great classical poet of Persia', yet he ranks highest amongst the more recent poets of modern Persia. His versatility was astonishing, for his prose works are as valuable as his poetry is good. In addition to three *díwáns* of lyrical poetry, many of which are after the style of Ḥáfiẓ, Jámí composed seven *maṣnawí* poems commonly grouped together, on the analogy of Niẓámí's *Khamsa* (Quintet) under the Arabic title of the *Saba'* (Septet), or of the Persian *Haft Awrang* (The Seven Thrones). The themes which the 'Septet' employs are ethical, mystical, allegorical, or romantic; they are not always original, and sometimes bear evident traces of the influence of Niẓámí, but the freshness of treatment which is their special characteristic has gained for them an enormous popularity. The occasional defects of Jámí's style, due to decadent influences, are displayed in his treatment of the best known *maṣnawí* of the seven, namely the *Yúsuf u Zulaykhá*. The story, that of Joseph and Potiphar's wife, was first used in verse by Firdawsí, and by comparison with the work of the master, Jámí's appears marred by much bombast and hyperbole and, most of all, by the predominant mysticism which entirely overshadows the story. It nevertheless has this advantage over Firdawsí's version, that it confines itself to the story of Yúsuf and Zulaykhá without detailing at great length the early history of Jacob, Joseph (Yúsuf) and the brothers.

For purposes of comparison each poet's version of the same incident (Zulaykhá's first approaches to Yúsuf) is appended. Firdawsí, who is the author of the first extract, describes how Yúsuf is distracted by grief at being separated from his father and how Zulaykhá attempts to console him by recounting all the possibilities of diversion open to him. Finally she declares her love:

If thy heart desires a loving heart,
A mistress that will be as thine own soul and as the whole world to thee,
Take me; for behold, I am thine.
I am thy worshipper and thy lover.
My heart, night and day, is the home of love for thee.
Day and night, mine eyes are upon thee:
Thou art the light in mine eyes,
Thou hast proved thyself the soul in my body,
For thee only I employ mind and reason,
For thine ends only do I work.
A pure body I keep everlastingly for thee,
Bound to thee I keep a loving heart.
Thine every command
I would carry out as a slave.

. . . .

Thus softly she spoke, and took him within her arms;
That she might take a kiss from his red lips.
But Yúsuf at this leapt to his feet
And took his hand from Zulaykhá's grasp.
And with shame his cheeks were blood-red.

. . . .

Then finally Yúsuf unloosed his tongue
And spoke thus: 'Gracious lady,
What corrupt thought and baseless plan do you entertain
In your unprofitable and unworthy words?
What wicked fancy hath possessed you?

. . . .

Jámí begins by generalizing:

When a beholder enters a garden
In his love for the rose his heart is charred like a tulip's.
First he is intoxicated at sight of the rose,
And, seeing, puts out his hand to pluck it.
Thus Zulaykhá sought means for her wooing,
But Yúsuf drew aside from her.
Zulaykhá's eyes shed tears of blood,
But Yúsuf fled from her.
Zulaykhá's soul was seared with pain,
But Yúsuf's heart was free from care.
Zulaykhá gazed in rapture upon his beauteous face,
But Yúsuf's glances were downward cast.
Zulaykhá burned with every glance,
But Yúsuf turned to avoid her eyes;
From fear of temptation he regarded not her face,
Nor looked upon her with temptation's eye.

Of Jámí's many prose works his *Ash'i'atu 'l Lama'át* (Rays of the Flashes) is a commentary on the mystical *Lama'át* of 'Iráḳí, which has been already mentioned. Amongst the best known of the others is a great dictionary of biographies of the Ṣúfí Saints, known as *Nafaḥátu 'l 'Uns* (The Breaths of Fellowship), and a further work connected with Ṣúfiism is his *Lawá'iḥ*, a short treatise on Ṣúfí doctrines with illustrative sections in verse. His *Bahláristán* (Abode of Spring) is perhaps the most popular of all his prose works, though from its large proportion of verse in it it may almost be called an anthology of poems. It was admittedly written in imitation of Sa'dí's *Gulistán*, and though, like its prototype, it was meant to amuse, it contains a number of serious biographies of the poets with quotations from their works. The *Bahláristán* does not in its style achieve the simplicity of the *Gulistán*. Particularly in the prose introductions to the various chapters there are visible the faults of overloaded rhetoric and ornate wording which were characteristic of most of the writings of the later Tímúrid period. These faults have been traced to foreign influence, and it is true that they appear at their worst, not in the writings of native Persians, but in those of Turks, Indians, and others to whom Persian was the language of literature rather than of everyday use. Foreign elements in Persia were important even under Tímúr, and multiplied enormously after his death.

Sultan Ḥusayn, the monarch under whom Jámí flourished, was the last of the Tímúrids in Persia. His kingdom did not go far beyond the confines of Harát. The south and west of Persia had never belonged to him, but had been divided up soon after Tímúr's death in A.D. 1405 between various Turkoman chiefs, who were for ever struggling with each other for supremacy. This state of anarchy, which endured for about a century, was ended by the rise of a Persian prince, who traced his descent from the seventh Imám of the Shí'a hierarchy, and who once more united the greater part of Persia under the sway of a native prince. This prince was Isma'íl, the founder of the Ṣafawí dynasty, whose members included the last of the powerful native rulers of Írán.

Modern Persia

THE Ṣafawí dynasty stands at the summit of one of the ever diminishing heights of power which distinguish the political history of Persia. It has particular significance from the fact that with it Persia became officially Shí'a, a step which had enormous political effect, though it merely brought to a head feelings which had long been dominant, and to which the literature of the land had constantly given expression. It was a contributory cause of the long struggles with Turkey that arose with the Ṣafawí sovereignty, and which resulted in the loss of much Persian territory to Turkey.

The characteristics of the latest period in Persia are an increase of intercourse with India and the countries of Europe, together with an enhanced religious consciousness. It is only with the nineteenth century that literature reflected these characteristics, but the signs are then unmistakable. In the preceding centuries literature for the most part followed the traditions of the great writers of Persia's past. These may be said to stand upon the crests of waves whose momentum set up series of smaller waves, each feebler than the last. The last great wave was capped by Jámí, but the movements perceptible in Persian literature of to-day are not of course exclusively due to Jámí's influence. They resemble the similar movements in all other countries, in that they are the result of the compounded impulses of all the native writers of the past who gave something new and original at rare intervals. The generous patronage of letters which permitted so much work to be done, and which was seen to so great advantage in Jámí's patron, became gradually rarer. Mír 'Alí Shír was not succeeded by another Maecenas in Persia until, a century later, the Ṣafawí Sháh 'Abbás the Great sat on the throne and gathered round him a group of writers who represented the best skill of the day in Persia. In India, where Bábur, the descendant of Tímúr, resuscitated the glories of the Mongol (or Moghul) dynasty, the encouragement of letters was more consistent and yielded greater results than in Persia. Bábur himself, while engaged in restoring the greatness of the Tímúrid house, found time to write his autobiography in the Turki language. His cousin, Mirzá Haydar Dughlát was the author of the *Ta'ríkh i Rashídi*, a valuable history of the Mongols of Central Asia.

But our business here is with the poets and other men of letters whose home was in Persia, who concerned themselves particularly with the affairs of their own country, and whose work is mainly the result of native patronage. Poetry in Persia did not die with Jámí. It would indeed have been strange if that branch of Persian letters had withered in which the native genius best expressed itself. Of the poets who followed Jámí, his nephew, Hátifí of Jám († 1521), is placed by such works as his *Laylá u Majnún*, *Khusraw u Shírín*, &c., in the front rank of the writers of romantic epic *maṣnawís*, while his purely epic work, as in his finely written *Tímúr-náma*, on the victories of Tímúr, gave new life to a form of poetry which had languished for centuries under the dull mediocrity of Firdawsí's many imitators. His work cannot claim to be equal to that of the master of epic. In fact he himself, in the preface to the *Tímúr-náma*, said that he could do better work if only he were freed from financial worries and allowed to devote himself to his art.

Occasionally there are graphic passages in the *Tímúr-náma*, of which the following is one describing the storming of a fortress :

> Flush with the sky was its topmost rampart,
> Whereon an angel might perch as a dove.
> They came leading lions, fortress-breakers,
> To storm that mighty golden fort of Náy.
> Upon all sides were wolves straining to attack,
> That against the ramparts set their efforts.
> Many a vessel of wood they builded
> To launch upon the waters of the moat.
> Like water-fowl upon the leaping waves
> They swam against the foot of that great wall.
> Nought they cared for any stone or arrow,
> And like the wind they sailed across the dike.
> From roof and rampart came the battle cry,
> While each and all did foam in angry toil.
> The sun was hidden in black clouds of dust,
> By rain of arrows was the aether pierced.
> First to raise his head in fight came Tímúr,
> And from the sea of courage took the pearl.
> On many a head great stones descended ;

For sign the prince bore a rope on his head.
By it the high wall a ladder became ;
On the wall's top it was tied in a noose.
At those fierce warriors' mighty attack,
The riddled wall changed to niched battlement.
Aloft they dashed against rampart and roof,
Drawing their swords to destroy all the foe.

Hátifí's contemporary Fighání, whose friend Jámí had been, lived for a time under the patronage of Sultán Ḥusayn. The jealousy of rivals brought about his departure from Harát to the court of the Áḳ Ḳuyunlu prince at Tabríz, where his merits were better appreciated and obtained for him the title of *Bábá i Shu'ará* (Father of the Poets). His particular merit lay in the fact that he ventured to introduce new methods of composition, and avoided the usual stereotyped similes in his verses; also, from his skill in the composition of odes he is sometimes called 'The Little Ḥáfiẓ. The date of the poet's death is variously given as 1516 or 1519.

Jámí's pupil Ásafí was, like himself, a protégé of Mír 'Alí Shír, whose notice he attracted by the elegance of his odes. His later contemporary Ahlí of Shíráz (1533) was an accomplished scholar as well as the writer of highly ingenious but artificial *ḳaṣídas*, the majority of them in praise of Sháh Isma'íl. An illustration of the importance attached to form in Persian poetry is provided by these poems, and by his *maṣ̤nawí* called *Siḥr i Ḥalál* (Lawful Magic). In this, the verses are so arranged that by following certain given indications the poem may be read in several different ways, each in a new metre and with the stress laid upon the mechanical construction rather than upon the sense. He was also inclined to mysticism, as is shown by his *Sham' u Parwána* (The Candle and the Moth), from which the following 'in praise of love' is an extract:

Happy the lover in whose generous fancy
His heart is the moth of the candle of beauty.
There flutters a moth in his bosom each evening:
Night finds him candle-like with burning heart waking.

Through his grief his heart like a burnt moth is tattered,
Like a candle his skirt with his tears is watered.
One may set to his heart, like a lantern, a brand,
That enflames his whole bosom at touch of the hand.
Of a kindling let no living heart be bereft,
Of what use is a candle that unlit is left? [1]

Another Ṣúfí contemporary with Ahlí was Hilálí of Astarabád. He was put to death in 1532 by the Uzbak conqueror of Harát, who had for a time befriended him, on the ground that he displayed Shí'a sympathies. A *díwán* of miscellaneous poems, a *maṣnawí* called *Sháh u Gadá* (The Prince and the Beggar), and an allegorical poem, *Ṣifátu 'l 'Áshiḳín* (Lovers' Attributes) exemplify the theosophical character of his work.

The worth of the poem *Sháh u Gadá* has been very variously estimated by European critics. It is said to have been much influenced by the mystical poem *Gúy u Chawgán* (The Ball and the Polo-stick), the author of which was Sháh-rukh's court-poet 'Árifí († A. D. 1449). According to Rieu, it contains none of the spiritual qualities of that work, whereas Ethé, who translated it into German, maintained that it is as full of mystical value as any work of the kind. To judge from the subject of the *maṣnawí* Rieu is right, for the story is that of the love of a prince for a dervish, which to our way of thinking is unreal material for a romantic poem. The Oriental mind, however, finds nothing repellent in the idea, and it is true that apart from the story the poem contains some fine passages, whereon doubtless Ethé based his approval.

Few men of mark in the literary history of Persia illumined the obscure years between the death of Sháh Isma'íl and the accession of Sháh 'Abbás. Sháh Isma'íl's son Sám Mírzá was responsible for a creditable piece of work called after him the *Tuḥfa i Sámí*, which was a series of bio-

[1] *Sham' u Parwána* (Bodley MS. Elliott 202, f. 14).

graphies continuing Dawlatsháh's work on the lives of the poets. Other names that occur are those of Ḥayratí († 1554), Sháh Ṭahmásp's chief poet, and Ḳásimí, the author of a *Sháh-náma* that recorded in verse the events of Sháh Isma'íl's reign and that of his successor. The latest and best known of all the poets of this period was Muhtasham Káshí († 1588), the panegyrist whose elegy on the martyrdom of Ḥusayn has provided one of the most eloquent manifestations of the Shí'a spirit known to Persian literature. An extract from it is given in Rizá Ḳulí Khán's great biographical work *Majma'u 'l Fuṣaḥá*, of which extract a prose translation is here attempted:

When that caravan reached the field of battle,
Uproar as of Judgement Day was added to the terror of their minds.
From six sides at once rose clamorous wailing for the dead;
Even upon the angels of the seven heavens weeping fell.
Where there was a gazelle it fled from the plain,
Where there was a bird it fell from the nest,
When its eyes beheld the bodies of the martyrs,
When its glance fell on the wounds made by arrow and spear.
Suddenly the glance of Zahrá [Fátima] in the midst of all
Fell upon the noble form of the Foremost of the Time;
Involuntarily burst the cry from her: 'This is Ḥusayn!';
As if it were a fire that fell upon earth from her.
Then with the tongue of lamentation, that incomparable virgin
Turned towards Madína crying: 'O Apostle of God,
This fallen one slain in the desert is thy Ḥusayn,
This prey to (men's) hands, with his feet deep in blood, is thy Ḥusayn.'[1]

Sháh 'Abbás the Great ascended the throne in A.D. 1587 and began a new era in the political history of Persia by his encouragement of intercourse with Europe. He received more than one embassy from the West and had an Englishman, Sir Anthony Shirley, as one of his ministers. In his own country his beneficent policy is shown to this day by the number of caravanserais called after him ''Abbásíyas'. He continued long-established custom by his patronage of letters, and his brilliant court at Isfahán included many

[1] Op. cit., vol. ii, p. 36.

panegyrists. Amongst these was Shání of Tihrán († 1614), who became famous not so much for the quality of his verse as by the fact that his sovereign rewarded him for one of his compositions by his weight in gold. Faṣíḥí of Harát († 1639), another panegyrist, had been at the court of the governor of Khurásán before entering the service of 'Abbás, and even the drunken Mírzá Jalál Asír, the Sháh's particular favourite, had some skill in letters. 'Abbás's physician Shifá'í († 1628) was also a satirist and a writer of original odes and *maṣnawís*. Of the latter four are known: *Mihr u Muḥabbat* (Love and Affection), *Namakdán i Ḥaḳíḳat* (The Salt-cellar of Truth), *Kiṣṣa' i 'Iráḳayn* (The Story of the Two Íráḳs)—after Kháḳáni's *Tuḥfatu 'l 'Iráḳayn*—and *Dída 'i Bídár* (The Wakeful Eye). The 'Salt-cellar of Truth' is a pious work written in praise of God's omniscience and omnipotence. Not a little of it is mystical, after the obscure style of the later Ṣúfís. For example:

O Thou the veil of Whose face is the curtain of phenomena,
From the sight even of Thy non-being cometh the brilliance of light.
When Thou dost go forward a pace,
Thou dost endow Thy path with splendour.
Thou that art the one king in splendour's palace
Dost desire naught and art paralleled by none.
Till Being raised its head through Thee
Chaos hastened to meet Chaos.
Thou didst come, none assisting Thee.
In past eternity Thou didst behold Thyself alone and none besides.
He that hath mind and reason doth understand
That there is no true servant of God but God Himself.
In Thy path reason seeth no advancement,
A pace or two it goeth and doth then return.[1]

The following quatrain is in a more characteristic ironical vein:

O mother mine, you are mother of one to whom
Nor his father's strength was known nor his mother's womb.
You say I have a sound body.—A thousand thanks!
You mean my body has naught within. Thanks to whom?[2]

Zulálí of Khwánsár († 1615–16) was another of the writers

[1] Bodley MS. Elliott 97, f. 69a.

[2] Op. cit., f. 472.

of *maṣnawís* who flourished under Sháh 'Abbás. His seven poems in that form, of which *Maḥmúd wa Ayáz*, the story of Sultán Maḥmúd and his slave Ayáz, is most often quoted, are grouped under the title of the *Sab' Sayyára*, or 'Seven Planets'. Other *maṣnawís* in the group are a mystical poem on the theme of Solomon and the Queen of Sheba, and another having Ḥasan as its hero. Some of the verse in *Maḥmúd wa Ayáz* reaches a high standard of poetry and much of it might well have been used in a work with a finer theme than that of this poem. Here is a passage introducing Maḥmúd at his evening prayers:

One night he remembered the Creator of his soul,
Disclosed the panorama of his heart.
For whether thou art in the 'ka'ba' or the tavern
Thou art still in the street of the Arbiter of thy needs.
Speak forth in the street of subtlety,
Read aloud the book of thy troubled heart.
His door has been made a collar for thee,
The custody of it is turned to a rent in thy skirt.
In any fashion strive, for in effort lies achievement;
Endeavour opens like a rose with success.
In that glorious Presence, before Whom is no 'Why?' nor 'How?',
Achievement is a fact approved.
When He unfastens, many a locked place is opened;
The locked door is the key to what is locked.
When He fastens a door, the opening thereof is with His own lock.
To fail in the task is more than the task itself.
Upon Him that needs no speech
The silent tongue prevails.
If a world come to His door without a gift
A tear is accounted as a caravan.
Shed a tear, for that banishes pain from thine eye.
The liver is more than the heart, and the heart more than the eye
    [i. e. Pain conquers love and love prevails over externals].
Whether it be prepared or not,
Everything in burning clings together like fire.
A heart without sorrow is an unlit lamp;
With the seal of death it is branded.[1]

It was natural that 'Abbás's court should be a stronghold of Shí'ism, and it sheltered at least one Shí'a divine, Baháu 'l Dín Ámulí († 1621). He is reckoned a standard

[1] Bodley MS. Elliott 269, f. 147.

authority on Shí'a law, having written at 'Abbás's request a treatise on that subject called *Jam' i 'Abbásí*. For a time he was Shaykhu 'l Islám; but he did not keep office for long, renouncing his position at court for a life of asceticism. Under the pen-name of 'Bahá'í' he composed a poem called *Nán u Ḥalwá*, or 'Bread and Sweets', in praise of his new life. According to Ethé it was intended as an introduction to the great *maṣnawí* of Rúmí.

'Abbás died in 1629, and his life and campaigns were celebrated in verse by a 'Sháh-náma' composed by Kamálí of Sabzawár, and in prose by a detailed history compiled by Iskandar Beg Munshí and known as *Ta'ríkh i Jahánárái 'Abbásí*, or 'History of 'Abbás, the World-Adorning'.

Mention cannot be altogether omitted of the writers who achieved fame in India at the Mughul courts, of whom many, particularly under the mighty Akbar, played a great part in Persian literature. Amongst those whose native land was Persia was the historian Khwándamír. He was the grandson of Mírkhwánd, who wrote the history known as *Rawẓatu 'l Ṣafá*, and was born at Harát. In India, where he went at the invitation of Bábur, he composed the *Ḥabíbu 'l Siyar* (The Friend of Biographies) which is his most extensive work. It is a general history of the world from the earliest times down to the death of Sháh Isma'íl Ṣafawí in A.D. 1524, and it concludes with an appendix on geography. The book shows traces of the influence upon the author of his grandfather's work, whereas he himself described it as an abbreviation of Sharafu 'l Dín's *Ẓafar-náma*. His other works, the *Khuláṣatu 'l Akhbár* (The Essence of History), the *Dastúru 'l Wuzará* (Model for Viziers), and the *Humáyún-náma*, though they are not marred by flowery verbosity in the same way as the *Ta'ríkh i Waṣṣáf*, for example, yet contain much that is high-flown and superfluous, and exhibit the corrupting foreign influences then prevalent. A valuable history, whose beginning was due to the emperor Akbar, was the *Ta'ríkh i Alfí* (Millennial Ḥistory), a chronological record of events during the millennium that followed the Prophet's death, set down by a number of hands.

Poets found great favour with Akbar. The lyricist Mushfiḳí of Bukhárá († A.D. 1586) and the *maṣnawí* writer Ḥusayn Ṣaná'í of Mashhad († A.D. 1588), owed much to him; but the principal poets of his reign were 'Urfí of Shíráz († A.D. 1590); the voluminous Fayẓí († A.D. 1595), whose works include an adaptation in Persian of an Indian romance entitled *Nal Daman*, after the style of Niẓámí's *Laylá u Majnún*; and Ẓuhúrí of Tihrán († A.D. 1616), who is best remembered for his *maṣnawí*, *Sáḳí-náma* (Book of the Cupbearer), imitated from a similar work by Ḥáfiẓ.

In the century or so that followed the death of Sháh 'Abbás the Great and before the end of the Ṣafawí dynasty, there were visible some traces of originality in the lucubrations of Persian authors. Ṣá'ib of Isfahán, who belonged to a family of Tabrízí origin, has been accounted the ablest Persian poet since Jámí. In early life he travelled extensively, and, after spending some time in India as court poet to the Mughul emperor Sháhjahán, he returned to Isfahán, where Shah 'Abbás II (reigned 1642–67) made him his laureate with the title of 'Maliku 'l Shu'ará' (King of the Poets). He is credited by native critics with the founding of a new school of poetry, and with having infused new life into the old forms that had been in use for centuries. His *díwán* includes many poems in the standard forms—odes, quatrains, panegyrics on various patrons, and a number of Turkish odes—his innovations made no lasting impression on his successors, in spite of any influence they may have had in his own day. The following ode is one taken at random from his collected works (Lucknow edition):

Man's struggle is to hold the reins of life.
'Breathe in tranquillity' is the constant counsel of the wise.
Thy life is past, and dost thou not modify thy words?
What dost thou achieve from this mill of thy teeth?
Thy rough lot will take to itself no file,
Unless the ups and downs of fortune are a file.
Life is destruction when the reins are taken from reason's hand.
The staff that from the hand of Moses fell, became a serpent.
If thou art a man, close the door in the face of desire;
Else 'twere easier to close up Alexander's wall.
Ṣá'ib, pour not forth thine honour [lit. water, (lustre) of face] for the sake of bread,
For the sum of honour is the water of life.

Ṣá'ib died in A.D. 1677. His contemporary, Fayyáẓ, reflected the national spirit in his *ḳaṣída* eulogizing the Imáms, and by his elegies on the tragic deaths of Ḥasan and Ḥusayn. He wrote in Arabic a work on metaphysics and Shí'a theology, and also a commentary in Persian on the *Fuṣúṣu 'l Hikam* (The Bezels of Philosophies) of the great Moorish mystic Ibnu 'l 'Arabí. The vizier of 'Abbás II, Ṭáhir Waḥíd, was an expert in the art of elegant letter-writing, technically known as *insḥá*, which is one of the recognized 'genres' of Persian literature; and he showed himself something of a historian in his *Ta'ríkh i Sháh 'Abbás i Ṣ̈ání* (History of Shah 'Abbás II). Towards the end of the Ṣafawí rule there flourished the poet Mír Abdu 'l 'Âl Naját († *c.* A.D. 1714) of Iṣfahán, whose *díwán* has been criticized by his contemporaries as being debased in its style and vulgar in its diction. On the other hand his *maṣnawí* on the art of wrestling, *Gul i Kushtí* (The Wrestling Gage, lit. The Rose of Wrestling) gained great favour and has found more than one commentator. In spite of its ostensible theme the poem contains very little on wrestling and is mainly of erotic content.

After the Ṣafawí period it begins to be apparent that, though the old forms of literary composition still remained in use, contact with the West and the rise of new influences had begun to bear fruit. One of the most brilliant of the Persian poets of the old style was the eighteenth-century writer Shaykh 'Alí Ḥazín, who was born at Isfahán and, after a busy youth spent in travel and literary composition, was compelled by political intrigue to flee to India. He was enormously prolific, writing, in addition to a large and useful biographical work, *Tazkiratu 'l Mu'áṣirín*, on the scholars and poets of his own day, an autobiography (*Tazkiratu 'l Aḥwál*), some memoirs on the campaigns of the Persian kings against India, seven *maṣnawís* and four *díwáns.* His work did not go uncriticized by his contemporaries, and doubtless with occasional justice, though it may be conceded that he had offended many members of his own craft by his indiscreet actions, with the almost inevitable result that his writings were bitterly attacked. He died at Benares in A.D. 1766.

In his native country the fame of Ḥazín is surpassed by that of Luṭf 'Alí Ázur, the author of the *Átash-kada* (Fire Temple). He was born at Isfahán of a noble family of Shámlu Turks, and spent some time in the service of the Afshárid Shahs (1736–96), who succeeded the Ṣafawís on the throne of Persia. He finally became a dervish and devoted himself to poverty and learning. His famous and constantly quoted biographical dictionary, the *Átash-kada*, was composed during the years 1760–77, and gives the lives of over eight hundred poets arranged under the headings of the towns or provinces in which they lived. His *díwán* includes many poems in all the usual forms, and his versatility is further displayed in a romantic *maṣnawí*, *Yúsuf and Zulaykhá.* The high standard set by him was not attained by his contemporary Fawḳí of Yazd, who began his poetical career in the ordinary way by writing eulogistic *ḳaṣídas*, odes on love and wine, and so forth. He found, however, that obscenity paid better, and, cynically attributing the debasement of his art to the lowered taste of the day, ended by becoming an apostle of vulgarity.

In the nineteenth century the Ḳájár sovereign, Fatḥ 'Alí Sháh (1797–1836), attempted a not very successful imitation of the 'Round Table' of Maḥmúd of Ghazna. He himself was something of a versifier, though his efforts were never even moderately good. His poet laureate, Fatḥ 'Alí Khán Ṣabá, composed a *díwán* and a *Sháhansháh-náma* in imitation of Firdawsí's classic work. But the official versifier was outdone in talent by Fatḥ 'Alí Sháh's Foreign Secretary, Abdu 'l Wahháb Nashát, whose *díwán* contains some excellent material, and who, in addition, wrote introductions in rhymed prose to the collected verses of his sovereign and to those of his colleague, the poet laureate. In his day, England, France, and Russia were competing with one another for political supremacy in Persia, and his correspondence, to judge from surviving specimens, was markedly skilful, though it did not lead to the best results for Persia. Another member of Fatḥ 'Alí's entourage was Mírzá Habíbu 'lláh († 1853), who is well known under the pen-name of Ḳá'ání. He is justly considered the most talented poet that Persia produced in the nineteenth century. Though his work does not contain the touches of genius which mark the work of the early classic poets, his satires and panegyrics have the unmistakable qualities of real poetry. He has the advantage, too, of a sense of humour, a quality deficient in some of his great predecessors; but this is too frequently overbalanced by a gloomy view of life.

An illustration of his pessimism is provided by the following fragment:

Upon thy talents rare 'twere vain,
My heart, to base a hope on earth;
The branch of talent or of skill
Bears naught but poverty and dearth.

'Tis useless quite in wisdom's tilth
To plant of hope the smallest seed;
That fruit may grow on branch of horn
Would be the most ill-founded creed.

Do not, to sate thy need for bread,
Favour the mean with flatt'ring glance;
And if in practice thou must cup,
To living veins apply thy lance.

Náṣiru 'l Dín Sháh (1848–96), who was nearly contemporary with Queen Victoria, and whose visits to England caused so much comment in the newspapers of the day, has some claim to notice as the author of widely-read diaries, which recount in simple Persian his experiences of the three journeys that he made to Europe. Of the professed men of letters that belonged to his reign the most notable was Riẓá Ḳulí Khán Lálá-Báshí († 1871). An able poet and the composer of lyrics, epics, and religious *maṣnawís*, he rendered valuable service to literary biography by his two great works, the *Majma'u 'l Fuṣaḥá* and the *Riyáẓu 'l 'Árifín*, which deal with the lives and works of Persia's men of letters from the beginnings of Persian literature down to the compiler's own day. For a time he was government representative at the court of the ruler of Khwárazm (Khwa). In his *Sifárat-náma* (Diary of a Mission) he gives an account of his journey to Khiva and of his mission there.

The direct influence of contact with Europe is visible in the work of Riẓá Ḳulí Khán's contemporary, Shaybání of Káshán. It reflects the pessimism and ultra-realism which was prevalent in European literature in the second half of the nineteenth century, and, though pessimism is no exotic growth in Persia—for even 'Umar Khayyám in the twelfth century preached it constantly—yet Shaybání's work is without the relieving quality of mysticism which characterized the followers of 'Umar. A different aspect of outside influences is revealed by a number of plays, for the most part comedies and all translated (many by Mírzá Ja'far, *v.*

list below) from Turkish originals, which bear evident traces of the influence of French literature. The popularity of these plays, none of which are ever performed, must be a restricted one, so long as it remains difficult to convince the Persian public that the spoken word, which is the fabric of all plays, can achieve the dignity of literature.[1]

In direct contrast to these secular and unacted plays of foreign origin are the *ta'ziyas*, or 'Passion Plays', that are acted every year in the month of Muḥarram as part of the mourning ceremonies for the martyrdom of Ḥusayn at Karbala and for the death of 'Alí and Ḥasan. These passion plays are the outcome of whatever national feeling exists in Persia. Political aspirations are held only by a small minority of the people, and amongst the bulk of the inhabitants any general and common aspirations have always been religious. The *ta'ziyas* give expression to this phase of national consciousness and concern themselves generally with the universally acknowledged saints and martyrs of Persia—'Alí, Ḥasan, and Ḥusayn—who are commonly endowed with god-like qualities.

The *ta'ziyas* are of quite modern origin, being apparently developed forms of the long elegies recited on the anniversary of the martyrdom at Karbala, or of the processions in which the Shí'a communities represent in rough tableaux the chief characters and incidents of that mournful occasion. Few of the 'plays' have been written down, and not many of their authors are known. For the most part only the main plot is given to the actors, who themselves fill it in by skilful improvisation. Often actors and audience are indistinguishable during representation of the plays,

[1] The following European editions have appeared:

(*a*) *The Vazir of Lankurán.* Haggard & Le Strange. London, 1882.

(*b*) *Trois Comédies traduites du dialecte turc 'Azeri' en persan . . . publiees . . . par Barbier de Meynard et S. Guyard.* Paris, 1886.

(*c*) *Three Persian Plays with . . . English translation . . .* by A. Rogers. London, 1890. [This reprints two plays from (*b*).]

which, both in the participants and spectators are capable of rousing the most violent religious emotion. The 'Kuláhís', or Europeanized 'cap-wearers', are nowadays inclined to belittle these representations, but they are still decidedly popular among the rank and file of the nation. Sir Lewis Pelly, who was the British Political Resident on the Persian Gulf in the second half of last century, published a translation of a *ta'ziya*, which he had 'collected from oral tradition'.[1] Some of its power to excite the feelings of a simple and fanatical people may be judged from the following portion of a scene taken from the play. The time is just after the mortal wounding of Ḥusayn:

Husain. Oh, how wounds caused by arrows and daggers do smart! O God, have mercy in the Day of Judgement on my people for my sake. The time of death has arrived, but I have not my Akbar with me. Would to God my grandfather the Prophet were now here to see me!

The Prophet (appearing). Dear Husain, thy grandfather the Prophet of God has come to see thee. I am here to behold the mortal wounds of thy delicate body. Dear child, thou hast at length suffered martyrdom by the cruel hand of my own people! This was the reward I expected from them; thanks be to God! Open thine eyes, dear son, and behold thy grandfather with dishevelled hair. If thou hast any desire in thy heart, speak it out to me.

Husain. Dear grandfather, I abhor life; I would rather go and visit my dear ones in the next world. I earnestly desire to see my companions and friends—above all, my dearly beloved son 'Ali Akbar.

The Prophet. Be not grieved that 'Ali Akbar thy son was killed, since it tends to the good of my sinful people on the day of universal gathering.[2]

The most significant religious movement of nineteenth-century Persia was the rise of Bábíism. It began in 1844, when Mírzá 'Alí Muḥammad of Shíráz proclaimed himself as the promised Mahdí and as the Báb, or 'Gate', through which alone 'Truth' might be gained. His teaching was

[1] Sir Lewis Pelly and A. N. Wollaston, *The Miracle Play of Hasan and Husain*, 2 vols., London, 1879.

[2] For *ta'ziyas* see further Le Comte de Gobineau, *Les Religions et les philosophies dans l'Asie Centrale*, Paris, 1865–6, and Matthew Arnold's Essay, 'A Persian Passion Play' (*Essays in Criticism*, 1st series).

a mystical and pantheistic theosophy that appears to be the outcome of Ṣúfiism, and was communistic and catholic in its application. Official Islám rose in immediate opposition to the movement, whose members were either killed, banished or persecuted in various cruel ways. Amongst the Báb's successors there has been a good deal of dispute concerning the exact line in which revelation has been transmitted. The largest number of Bábís attached themselves to Baháu 'lláh, after whom the movement is often called Baháism. The value of Bábism is historical rather than literary, for it is an illustration of the mode in which religions are formed. But it is not entirely devoid of literary interest. The Báb himself wrote several treatises, of which the most important is the *Bayán* (Explanation), to expound his doctrines. His successors and the rival claimants to his mantle have contributed a number of works, mainly apologetics, to the literature of the movement. The question whether Bábism is destined for future greatness in Persia must remain difficult to answer while Islám, through the enormous influence of the '*Ulamá*, the religious leaders, retains its hold on the people. The movement, which has found a sympathetic historian in Professor E. G. Browne, certainly indicates a possibility of renewed spiritual life. Meantime, while Persia is politically engaged in a struggle to find some congenial form of government and some method of reconciling her aims with those of her neighbours—with unfortunate results for her—intellectually she shows some few signs of vigour. The ideas of patriotism and nationality, which are the result of imported Western education, have led to the glorification of any works like the *Sháh-náma* which contain elements of national interest. On the other hand, the Ṣúfís and mystics who supplied what was, judging by ordinary canons, the best and most universally appreciated in Persian poetry, are falling into disrepute. They are condemned for having discouraged the exercise of the human will and for causing national degeneracy by their teaching of quietism and submission. For the most part the work of twentieth-century Persian littérateurs is published in newspapers and other journals whose aims are mainly political. The *Siyáḥat-náma'i Ibrahím Beg* (The Diary of Ibrahím Beg's Travels) is an exception. It was written by Hájjí Zaynu 'l 'Ábidín, a merchant of Kurdistán whose family came originally from Marágha. In the course of his business travels he made long stays in the Caucasus and the Crimea and at Stambúl, and in the *Siyáḥat-náma* he provided a readable account, in prose, of his wanderings. The book was published at Calcutta in 1910, the year of the author's death.

The contributors to ephemeral journals are treated at length in Professor Browne's *Press and Poetry of Modern Persia* (Cambridge, 1914). Amongst the best known of them is Bahár, who is an attendant at the shrine of Imám Riẓá at Mashbad and founder of a newspaper in that holy city. Another is 'Ásif of Ḳazwín, a writer of political ballads who has suffered imprisonment for his views, and, finally, there is the poet Sayyid Ashraf of Gílán who has distinguished himself by his poems criticizing the reactionary *mullás*. These are amongst the few inhabitants of Persia for whom intellectual life has any meaning. What promise of spiritual vitality exists in the great mass of the people must remain unfulfilled until the country frees itself from the shackles of mediaevalism in which it is now fettered.

A List of Modern General Works, Persian Texts, and Translations published mainly in Europe.

The following list makes no claim to completeness, and is intended merely to indicate the most accessible of the works required for the further study of Persian literature. For Oriental and other editions of texts the *British Museum Catalogue of Persian Printed Books*, 1922, should be consulted; for MSS., the catalogues of C. Rieu and H. Ethé.

Note.—Books printed in Muḥammadan countries bear a date of the Muḥammadan era (A.H. = the year of the Flight, *hijra*), which began in A.D. 622. It must be borne in mind, when calculating a date A.D. from a date A.H., that the Muslim year is eleven days shorter than ours.

I. SOME RECENT GENERAL CRITICAL WORKS RELATING TO THE LITERATURE, HISTORY, LANGUAGE, GEOGRAPHY, &c., OF PERSIA.

E. G. Browne. *A Literary History of Persia.* 2 vols. London, 1906, 1908.

—— *Persian Literature under Tartar Dominion, A.D. 1265–1502.* Cambridge, 1920.

The standard works in English on the subject. A most valuable conspectus of Persian literature from the earliest times down to A.D. 1502. Vol. i contains an excellent bibliography of general works.

W. Geiger and E. Kuhn. *Grundriss der Iranischen Philologie.* 2 vols. Strassburg, 1896–1904. An encyclopaedia of Iranian philology, literature, and history. The various sections contain complete bibliographies.

P. Horn. *Geschichte der Persischen Literatur.* Leipzig, 1901.

G. Le Strange. *The Lands of the Eastern Caliphate.* Cambridge, 1905.

E. G. Browne. *The Press and Poetry of Modern Persia.* Cambridge, 1914.

Sir Percy Sykes. *A History of Persia.* 2 vols. London, 1st ed. 1915, 2nd ed. 1921.

II. OLD PERSIAN. TEXTS, &c.

Fr. Spiegel. *Die Altpersischen Keilinschriften im Grundtexte, mit Uebersetzung, Grammatik und Glossar.* Leipzig, 1862 and 1881.

C. Kossowicz. *Inscriptiones Palaeo-Persicae Achaemenidarum.* St. Petersburg, 1872.

L. W. King and R. Campbell Thompson. *The Sculptures and Inscriptions of Darius the Great on the Rock of Behistun in Persia.* London, 1907.

H. C. Tolman. *Ancient Persian Lexicon and Texts* (1908) and *Cuneiform Supplement* (1910), being vols. vi and vii of the Vanderbilt Oriental Series. The Vanderbilt University, U.S.A.

Avesta.

J. Darmesteter and L. H. Mills. *The Zend-Avesta.* In vols. iv, xxiii, and xxxi of *The Sacred Books of the East.* Oxford, 1895 (2nd ed. of Part I), 1883, and 1887.

J. Darmesteter. *Le Zend-Avesta: Traduction nouvelle avec commentaire historique et philologique.* 3 vols. Paris, 1892–3.

III. GENERAL WORKS ON ZOROASTRIANISM, &c.

A. V. Williams Jackson. *Zoroaster, the Prophet of Ancient Iran.* New York, 1899.

—— *Persia, Past and Present.* New York, 1906.

IV. PAHLAWI WORKS. TEXTS, TRANSLATIONS, &c.

E. W. West, M. Haug, &c. *The Book of Arda Viráf:* Pahlawi text . . . with an English Translation and Introduction. Bombay and London, 1874.

E. W. West. *The Mainyo i Khard* (*or Spirit of Wisdom*) . . . in Roman characters . . . with an English translation, &c. Stuttgart and London, 1871.

—— Pahlawi texts, translated in vols. v, xviii, xxiv, xxxvii, and xlvii of *The Sacred Books of the East.*

V. WORKS ON ISLÁM, CRITICAL INTRODUCTIONS TO LITERATURE, HISTORIES, &c.

S. Lane-Poole. *Mohammadan Dynasties.* London, 1894.

R. A. Nicholson. *Studies in Islamic Mysticism.* Cambridge, 1921.

—— *Studies in Islamic Poetry.* Cambridge, 1921.

—— *Translations of Eastern poetry and prose.* Cambridge, 1922.

—— *The Kashf al-Maḥjúb, the oldest Persian treatise on Ṣúfiism, by al-Hujwírí, translated by R. A. Nicholson.* E. J. W. Gibb. Memorial Series, vol. xvii. London, 1911.

VI. A LIST OF PERSIAN AUTHORS, with their printed works in the original or in translation, arranged according to the alphabetical order of their usual appellations.

Abú Sa'íd ibn Abí 'l Khayr. *Quatrains.* Assembled and translated by H. Ethé in *Sitzungsberichte der bayrischen Akademie*, philos.-philolog. Klasse, 1875 and 1878.

Anwarí ('Alí Awḥadu 'l Dín). Oriental lithographed editions only, of which the latest is the Lucknow edition of 1889.

'Aṭá Malik i Juwayní ('Aláu 'l Dín 'Aṭá Malik). *The Ta'ríkhi-i-Jahán-Gushay of 'Aláu 'd din 'Aṭá Malik-i-Juwayni.* Part I. Containing the history of Chingiz Khan and his successors, ed. with an introd. . . . by Mirza Muhammad . . . Qazwíní (and E. G. Browne). E. J. W. Gibb Memorial Series, vol. xvi. London, 1912.

—— Part II. *The History of the Khwarazmshahs.* London, 1917.

Avicenna (Abú 'Alí ibn Síná). *Dánish-náma i 'Alá'í.* Lithographed edition. Hyderabad, A.H. 1309.

Badawání. *Muntakhabu 'l Tawáríkh.* Ed. W. N. Lees, &c. Calcutta, 1864–8.

al Bal'amí. *Chronique . . . de Tabari*, traduite sur la version persane de . . . Bel'ami . . ., par M. Hermann Zotenberg. 4 vols. Paris, 1867–74.

Dawlatsháh. *The Tadhkiratu 'sh-shu'ará (Memoir of the Poets) of Dawlatshah bin 'Alá u'd-Dawla . . . of Samarqand.* Ed. . . . by E. G. Browne. Persian Historical Texts, vol. i. London, 1901.

Farídu 'l Dín 'Aṭṭár (Muḥammad ibn Ibrahím). *Pend-Nameh*, ou le livre des conseils en persan, et traduit par S. de Sacy. Paris, 1819.

—— *Mantic Uttair*, ou le langage des oiseaux; poème de philosophie religieuse publié en Perse par Garcin de Tassy. Paris, 1857.

—— . . . trad. du persan par G. de Tassy. Paris, 1863.

Tadhkiratu 'l Awliya (Memoirs of the Saints) of Muḥammad ibn Ibrahím Faríd u'ddín 'Aṭṭár. Ed. in the original Persian by R. A. Nicholson. Persian Historical Texts, vols. iii and iv. London, 1905–7.

Firdawsí. *Sháh-náma.*

Turner Macan. *The Shah nameh.* 4 vols. Calcutta, 1829. 8vo.

Julius Mohl. *Le Livre des Rois.* 7 vols. Paris, 1838–78. Folio (with translation in French facing the Persian text).

Vullers. *Firdusi Liber Regum* . . . Tom. 1–3. Lugduni Batavorum, 1877–84. 8vo.

Mohl. *Le Livre des Rois* . . . 7 vols. Paris, 1877–8. Small 8vo. A French translation in prose extracted from the greater work, and published separately.

Italo Pizzi. *Firdusi. Il Libro dei Rei.* 8 vols. Torino, 1886–8, A metrical translation in Italian.

Abridgments, Selections, &c.

J. Atkinson. *The Shah Nameh* . . . Translated and abridged. London, 1832.

Friedrich Rückert. *Firdosi's Königsbuch* . . . Übersetzt von Friedrich Rückert. Berlin, 1890–4.

I. Pizzi. *Antologia Firdusiana.* Leipzig, 1891.

Yúsuf and Zalîkhâ. Ed. by H. Ethé. Anecdota Oxoniensia. Oxford, 1908.

Ḥáfiẓ (Shamsu 'l Dín Muḥammad). *The Díwán.* Ed. H. Brockhaus. Leipzig, 1854–6.
Ed. and translated by Vincenz Ritter von Rosenzweig-Schwannau. 3 vols. Vienna, 1856–1864.
Translated by H. Wilberforce Clarke. 2 vols. London, 1891.
Selections. Translated by H. Bicknell. London, 1875.
Ḥamdulláh Mustawfí Ḳazwíní. *Ta'ríkh i Guzída—or Select History.* With an introd. by E. G. Browne. Vol. i, text. E. J. W. Gibb Memorial Series. Vol. xiv. 1. London, 1910.
Vol. ii, abridged translation by E. G. Browne. London, 1914.
—— *Nuzhatu 'l Qulúb.* Ed. G. Le Strange. London, 1913.
—— *Nuzhatu 'l Qulúb.* Trans. G. Le Strange. London, 1918. E. J. W. Gibb Memorial Series, vol. xxiii. 1, 2.
Hátifí of Jám. *Tímúr-náma.* Lithographed under the title of *Ẓafar-náma i Hátifí.* Lucknow, 1869.
Ḥazín. *Collected Works.* Lucknow ?, 1876.
Ḥilálí. *Díwán.* Cawnpore. 1881 and 1888.
Ḥusayn Wá'iẓ Káshifí. *Anvari Suheli, or Lights of Canopus, being the Persian version of the Fables of Bidpai.* Ed. by J. W. Ouseley. Hertford, 1851.
—— *Anvari Suhaili* ... Translated by E. B. Eastwick. Hertford, 1854.
—— *The Anwár-i-Suhaili . . . commonly known as Kalilah and Damnah* ... Trans. ... by A. N. Wollaston. London, 1877.
—— *Akhlak i Muhsini.* Translated by H. G. Keene. Hertford, 1851.
Ibrahím Beg. *Siyahat-náma'i Ibrahim Beg.* Edited by D. C. Phillott and Md. Kázim Shírází. Calcutta, 1910.
Jalálu 'l Dín Rúmí (Muḥammad ibn Muḥammad Balkhi). *Maṣnawí-i-Ma'nawí.* Oriental editions. Bombay, A.H. 1280; Lucknow, A.H. 1282 and 1291; (with Turkish translation) Bulak, A.H. 1268.
—— *Masnavi i Ma'navi* . . . Translated and abridged by. E. H. Whinfield. 2nd ed. London, 1898.
—— *The Mesnevi* ... book the first . . . translated and the poetry versified by J. W. Redhouse. London, 1881.
—— *The Masnavi* ... Book 2. Translated into prose by C. E. Wilson. 2 vols. London, 1910.
—— *Mesnevi oder Doppelverse des Scheich Mewlana Dschelal ed din Rumi.* ... aus dem Persischen übertragen von Georg Rosen, mit einer Einleitung von Fr. Rosen. New edition. München, 1913.
—— *Dīvāni Shamsi Tabrīz.* Selected poems, edited and translated by R. A. Nicholson. Cambridge, 1898.
Jámí (Mullá Núru 'l Dín 'Abdu 'l Raḥmán). *Beharistan oder Frühlingsgarten* . . . übertragen von Schlechta-Wssehrd. Vienna, 1846.
—— *The Beharistan (Abode of Spring).* A literal translation from the Persian. Printed by the Kama Shastra Society. Benares, 1887. (Poor and inaccurate.)

Jámí (Mullá Núru 'l Dín Abdu 'l Raḥmán). *Lawá'iḥ. A Treatise on Ṣúfiism*. . . Facsimile of an old MS. With a translation by E. H. Whinfield. London, 1906 and 1914.

—— *Nafaḥátu 'l Uns . . . or the lives of the Ṣufis.* Ed. by Mawlawis Gholam 'Iisa 'Abd al Hamid, &c. With a biographical sketch of the author by W. Nassan Lees. Calcutta, 1859.

—— *Risálat.* A treatise on Persian rhyme . . . Ed. by H. Blochmann. Calcutta, 1867.

—— *Salámán and Absál*: rendered into English verse by Edward Fitzgerald. London, 1879, 1904, &c.

—— *Yúsuf u Zulikha.* Ed. with German translation by Rosenzweig. Vienna, 1820.

—— *Yusuf and Zulaikha*: a poem translated from the Persian into English verse by R. T. H. Griffith. London, 1882.

—— *The Book of Joseph and Zuleikha* . . . Historical romantic Persian poem. Translated into English verse by Alexander Rogers. . . . London, 1892 and 1910.

—— *Tuḥfatu 'l Aḥrár* (*The Gift of the Noble*). Ed. by F. Falconer. London, 1848.

Ḳá'ání. *Selections from Qāāni* . . . Ed. by Muḥammad Kázim Shírází under the supervision of Lt.-Col. D. C. Phillott. Calcutta, 1907.

Kay Káus ibn Iskandar. *The Ḳábus-náma.* Persian text ed. by Riẓá Ḳuli Khan. Teheran, A.H. 1285.

—— *The Ḳábus-náma.* Traduit par A. Querry. Paris, 1886.

—— *The Ḳábus-náma.* Übersetzt von H. F. von Diez. Berlin, 1811.

Kháḳání. Oriental lithographed editions of the complete works. Lucknow, 1876, 1879.

—— *Tuḥfatu 'l 'Iráḳayn.* Lucknow, 1876.

Khwándamír (Ghiyaṣu 'l Dín ibn Humá mu 'l Dín). *Habíbu 'l Siyar.* Lithographed editions. Teheran, A.H. 1270–4; Lucknow, A.D. 1883.

First two volumes translated by E. Rehatsek and T. F. Arbuthnot in New Oriental Translation Fund Series. 5 vols. London, 1891–4.

—— *A History of the Minor Dynasties of Persia*, being an extract from the *Habíb-us-siyar* of Khondamir. Ed. by G. S. A. Ranking. London, 1910.

Maḥmúd Shabistarí. *Gulshan i Ráz.* Persisch u. deutsch herausgegeben von Hammer-Purgstall. Leipzig, 1838.

—— Translated with introduction, &c., by E. H. Whinfield. London, 1880.

Minuchihrí. A. de Biberstein-Kasimirski: Menoutchehri . . . texte, traduction, notes, et introduction historique. Paris, 1886.

Mír Abdu 'l 'Ál Naját. *Gul u Kushtí.* Lucknow, 1881.

Mírkhwánd (Muḥammad ibn Kháwand Sháh). *Rawẓatu 'l Ṣafá.*

(*a*) *Histoire des Samanides*: texte persan, traduit etc. . . . par M. Defrémery. Paris, 1845.

(*b*) *Historia Gasnevidarum*, persice . . . latine vertit Frid. Wilker. Berlin, 1832.

(c) *Historia Seldschukidarum . . .* persice . . . germanice ed. etc. J. A. Vullers. Giessen, 1837.
(d) *The History of the Atabeks of Syria* . . . Ed. W. H. Morley. London, 1848.
(e) *History of the Early Kings of Persia.* Trans. by David Shea. London, 1832.

Naját (Mír Abu 'l 'Al). *Guli Kushtí.* Lithographed, Lucknow, 1881.

Náṣiri Khusraw. *Safar Nameh. Relation du voyage de Nasiri Khusrau en Syrie,* etc. . . . Publ. des langues orientales vivantes, Série 2, vol. i. Paris, 1881.

Náṣiru 'l Dín Sháh. The Diary of H.M. the Shah of Persia during his tour through Europe in A.D. 1873. Translated by J. W. Redhouse. London, 1874.

—— A second tour in Europe, 1878. Translated by A. Houtoum Schindler and Baron Louis de Norman. London, 1879.

Naṣíru 'l Dín Ṭúsí. *Akhlaḳi Náṣirí.* Oriental editions: Lucknow, A.H. 1286; Lahore, A.D. 1865.

Niẓámí-i-'Arúẓí-i-Samarkandi. *Chahár Maqála.* Edited by Mirza Muhammad of Qazwin. E. J. W. Gibb Memorial Series. Vol. xi. London, 1910.

—— Revised translation of the *Chahár Maqála* (*Four Discourses*) . . . by E. G. Browne. E. J. W. Gibb Memorial Series, vol. xi. 2. London, 1921.

Niẓámi of Ganja (Ilyás ibn Yúsuf). *Laili and Majnun. . .* From the original Persian by J. Atkinson. London, 1836; reprinted, London, 1894.

—— *Makhzan ul Asrár, the Treasury of Secrets.* Ed. by N. Bland. London, 1844.

—— *Khirad Námahi Iskandary* . . . Ed. by A. Sprenger and others. Calcutta, 1852–69 (vol. xvii, ser. 3, of the Bibliotheca Indica).

—— *The Sikandar Nama* . . . Trans. by H. B. Clarke. London, 1881.

Niẓámu 'l Mulk. *Siyásat-náma.*
Siyasat Nameh. Traité de gouvernement composé pour le Sultan Melik-Chah par le vizir Nizam oul Moulk. Texte persan éd. par C. Schefer. (Publications de l'École des langues orientales vivantes, Série 3, vol. vii.)
Traduit par C. Schefer (as above, vol. viii). Paris, 1891–7.

Rashídu' l Dín Fazlu 'lláh. E. Quatremère: *Histoire des Mongols, etc.* Tome I. Paris, 1836. (Gives the history of Húlágú Khan out of the *Jámi'u' l Tawáríkh.*)

—— *Djami el Tawarikh . . . Histoire générale du monde par Fadl Allah Rashid ed Din . . . Histoire des Mongols,* éd. par E. Blochet. E. J. W. Gibb Memorial Series, vol. xviii. London, 1911.

Riẓá Ḳulí Khán (Lálá-Báshí). *Majma'u 'l Fuṣaḥá.* 2 vols. Teheran, 1877.

—— *Riyáẓu 'l 'Árifín.* Lithographed, Teheran, A.H. 1305.

—— *Sifárat-náma'i Khwárazm.* Teheran, A.H. 1292. Paris, A.D. 1879.

Rúdagí. A complete edition of extant poems with German translation in *Göttinger Nachrichten*, 1873, pp. 663–742.

Sa'dí (Musliḥu 'l Dín Sa'dí Shírází). *Le Boustan*, texte persan, avec un commentaire persan . . . par C. H. Graf. Vienne, 1858.

—— *The Bustan* . . . Photographed from a MS. prepared under the superintendence of J. T. Platts . . ., annotated by A. Rogers. London, 1891.

—— *The Bustan* . . . Translated . . . into prose . . . by W. H. Clarke. London, 1879.

—— *The Garden of Fragrance*: a complete translation of the Bostan of Sadi . . . into English verse by G. S. Davie. London, 1882.

—— *With Sadi in the Garden: or the book of love*: being the Ishk or third chapter of the *Bostan* of the Persian poet Sadi embodied in a dialogue held in the garden of the Taj Mahal at Agra, by Sir Edwin Arnold. 3rd ed. London, 1888.

—— *The Gulistan*. A new edition by E. B. Eastwick. Hertford, 1850.

—— *The Gulistan*. A new edition by John Platts. London, 1871 and 1874.

—— *The Gulistan: or Rose Garden*. Translated by Francis Gladwin. London, 1808.

—— *The Gulistan: or Rose Garden*. Translated into prose and verse . . . by E. B. Eastwick. 2nd ed. London, 1880.

—— *The Gulistan*. Translated, with notes, by J. T. Platts. London, 1873.

Ṣá'ib. *Collected Works*. Lucknow, 1880.

Saná'í of Ghazna (Abu' l Majd Majdúd ibn Adaní). *Ḥadíḳatu 'l Ḥaḳíḳa*. Lithographed edition. Lucknow, 1886.

—— *The First Book of the Hadiqatu'l Haqiqat, or the Enclosed Garden of the Truth*. . . Edited and translated by Major J. Stephenson. (Bib. Indica.) Calcutta, 1911.

Sharafu 'l Dín 'Alí Yazdí. *Ẓafar-náma*, in Bibliotheca Indica. Calcutta, 1885–8.

Ṭáhir Waḥíd. *Letters*. Lucknow, 1873.

'Umar Khayyám. *The Text and Translation of the oldest MS. of the quatrains ascribed to 'Umar Khayyám*. E. H. Allen. London, 1898.

—— *The Multi-Variorum Edition of 'Umar Khayyam*. N. Haskell Dole. London, 1889. [Enumerates most of the European versions.]

'Unṣurí (Abú 'l Ḳásim Ḥasan). Teheran, A.H. 1298.

'Urfí. *Ḳaṣídas*. Cawnpore, A.D. 1880.

'Utbi. *Ta'ríkhi Yamíní* in the Arabic original. Ed. A. Sprenger. Delhi, 1847.

—— *Tarjumai Yamíní*, the Persian version of the above, translated by J. Reynolds, in Oriental Trans. Fund Series. London, 1858.

Waṣṣáf (Shiháb u'l Din 'Abdullah Shírází). *Ta'ríkhi Waṣṣáf*. Lithographed. Bombay, A.H. 1269.

Zulálí. *Maḥmúd u Ayáz*. Lithographed edition. Lucknow, A.H. 1290.

LIST OF AUTHORS

The main references are given by the numerals in heavy type.

Printed in England at the Oxford University Press

Dr. B. J. Karlgren (Professor of Sinology in the University of Göteborg, Sweden), Mr. A. A. Macdonell (Boden Professor of Sanskrit, Oxford), Mr. T. Nicklin (Warden of Hulme Hall, Manchester), Mr. Kenneth Sisam (editor of *Havelok the Dane* and *Fourteenth-Century Prose and Poetry*), Mr. J. R. R. Tolkien (Reader in English Language in the University of Leeds), Mr. G. van Santvoord (Lecturer in English in Yale University), Dr. Johan Vising (Professor of Romance Languages in the University of Göteborg, Sweden), Dr. L. Willoughby (Lecturer in German in the University of Sheffield).

¶ *The following volumes have appeared*

The Pronunciation of English reduced to Rules by means of a system of Marks applied to the Ordinary Spelling. By W. A. Craigie, M.A., LL.D. 52 pp. 1*s.* 9*d.* net.

"Dr. Craigie has ingeniously, and without too many or too difficult diacritical marks, produced a small and workmanlike handbook."—*The Athenæum.*

"Le système proposé offre l'avantage de fixer dès le début l'attention de l'élève sur l'orthographe des mots, qu'il lui faudra bien arriver à connaître, de toute façon."—*Revue de l'Enseignement des Langues Vivantes.*

On the Relations between Spoken and Written Language with special reference to English. By Henry Bradley, M.A., Hon. D.Litt. Oxon., F.B.A. 36 pp. 2*s.* net. (Reissued by the courtesy of the British Academy.)

"This little book deserves to be read carefully by spelling reformers of all degrees, for it will give them plenty to think about. . . . It goes deeper down into the philosophy of the English language than much that is written or said about it."—*The Times.*

"By shaking up some of our fixed ideas on the mental effect of our established ways of spelling and printing words, Dr. Bradley calls attention to the actualities of the problem of spelling reform, corrects general misconceptions, and puts the case in a clearer light."—*The Athenæum.*

Epochs of Italian Literature. By Cesare Foligno, M.A. 96 pp. 3*s.* net.

"This small volume . . . is a really remarkable achievement. . . . A very good bibliography and reference index add to the usefulness of the volume."
The Journal of Education.

"This is a most valuable work. . . . The book is one which even the scholar familiar with the most elaborate histories of Italian literature will find it profitable to read; whilst to the beginner it offers such a sketch of the whole wide field as he will find nowhere else."—*The Author.*

"He has as much to tell us about the Futurists as about Dante, and rightly so, for it is almost as hard to get sound sense about the Futurists as it is easy to get good information about Dante."—*The Athenæum.*

The Sounds of Standard English with some Notes on Accidence and Syntax. By T. Nicklin, M.A. 102 pp. 3*s.* net.

"This book is a joy to the reader. The writer has the lighter touch without sacrificing any of his scholarship. He knows his subject and succeeds in making it very human and attractive. We doubt if any reader will leave the book until it is read from cover to cover."—*The Educational Times.*